THE
ENCYCLOPEDIA
OF
EMBROIDERY
TECHNIQUES

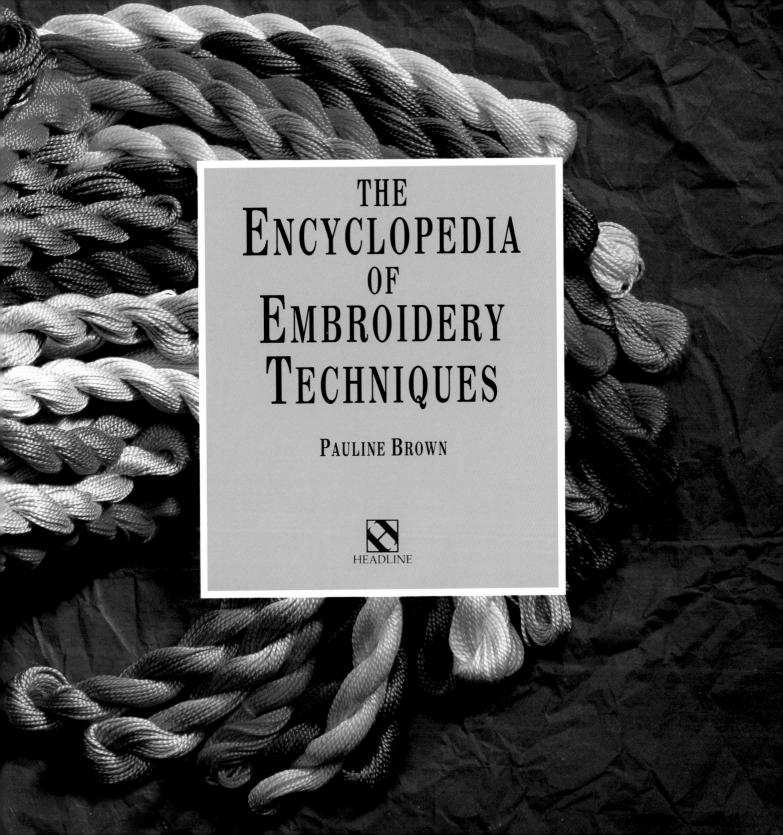

THE ENCYCLOPEDIA OF EMBROIDERY TECHNIQUES

Pauline Brown

HEADLINE

A QUARTO BOOK

Copyright © 1994 Quarto Publishing plc
First published in Great Britain in 1994 by
HEADLINE BOOK PUBLISHING

10 9 8 7 6 5 4 3 2 1

HEADLINE BOOK PUBLISHING
A division of Hodder Headline plc
338 Euston Road
London NW1 3BH

British Library Cataloguing in Publication Data

Brown, Pauline
  Encyclopedia of Embroidery Techniques
  I. Title
  746.44

  ISBN 0-7472-0980-4

This book was designed and produced by
Quarto Publishing plc
6 Blundell Street
London N7 9BH

Senior art editor Amanda Bakhtiar
Designer Kathy Gummer
Illustrators Elsa Godfrey, Rob Shone
Embroidery samples Jane Dew of The Creative
Company
Photographers Sue Baker, Chas Wilder
Picture researcher Emma Enthoven
Senior editor Hazel Harrison
Copy editors Hazel Harrison, Michele Clark
Editorial director Sophie Collins
Art director Moira Clinch

Typeset by Genesis Typesetting, Rochester, Kent
Manufactured by Regent Publishing Services Ltd.,
Hong Kong
Printed in China

CONTENTS

MAKING A START

Embroidery in the late 20th century has come a long way from the traditions of the past. However, the basic methods still hold good – without sound technique and suitable materials and equipment embroiderers are unlikely to be able to exploit their ideas to create exciting and innovative work.

Most people manage with quite a small basic kit of tools: scissors, pins and needles, tape measure and embroidery frame, and these, together with an iron and a sewing machine, are all that are needed to make a start.

Needles
It is essential to choose a needle which suits both the fabric and thread and the type of embroidery you are undertaking. The needle should pass easily through the fibres of the fabric, and the yarn through the eye of the needle. Needle size is designated by number, with the lowest number in each category signifying the longest and thickest.

Embroidery (or crewel) needles in sizes 1–10 have long eyes which will take embroidery silks, cottons and linens, and fine wools. They are suitable for a wide range of embroidery techniques.

Quilting needles, also known as ''betweens'', and made in sizes 1–10, are short with small round eyes. They are ideal for making the quick, even stitching needed for techniques such as quilting and hemming in fine thread.

Chenille needles, in sizes 13–24, have sharp points and large eyes, and will take all types of thick yarn as well as ribbon and raffia.

Tapestry needles are similar to chenilles, and also come in sizes 13–24, but have blunt points which slip between the threads of canvas or the fibres of evenweave linen, making them the correct choice for needlepoint and all the counted thread methods.

Other specialist needles include long, fine *beading needles*, and *leather needles* whose triangular points will pierce all types of leather, suede or plastic.

Bodkins are for threading elastic, ribbons and cords, while *circular needles* are good for three-dimensional embroidery.

Threads
Good-quality thread and yarns are essential, and they should be selected not only for practical reasons but also for aesthetic ones: colour and texture are both vital factors in embroidery.

There are so many different types of thread on the market today that the choice may at

Circular needles

Chenille needles

Bodkins

Embroidery or crewel needles

Darners

Tapestry needles

Quilting needles

Beading needles

Leather needles

Metallic
threads

Pearl
cotton

Tapestry wools in 2-, 3-, 4-ply

first be overwhelming. Indeed anything which can be threaded through the eye of a needle can be put to use in an imaginative way for experimental work. Besides conventional embroidery threads, knitting and crochet yarns, ribbons and cords are also readily available, while some of the more specialist items can be purchased by mail order.

Cotton threads in a range of colours and thicknesses are widely used for all types of embroidery, as they are hard-wearing and washable. Stranded cotton is particularly versatile because the six strands can be divided to produce a number of thicknesses. This makes it suitable for different effects and techniques, particularly for surface stitches. For counted thread work, changes of tone can be achieved by varying the number of strands. In needlepoint, cotton can add lustre to contrast with the matt texture of the more usual woollen threads.

Pearl cotton (perlé) is a shiny, twisted yarn which comes in balls and skeins in three thicknesses – 3, 5 and 8. It is suitable for surface embroidery and needlepoint as well as coarser types of counted thread work.

Coton à broder has a slight sheen and is of fine twisted construction. It is particularly good for counted thread techniques and smocking as there are no strands to separate.

Soft embroidery thread is a thick cotton yarn with a matt surface; it can be used for needlepoint and work on coarsely woven fabrics.

Embroidery wools come in several qualities and thicknesses. Although some are primarily manufactured for needlepoint, they are suitable for all types of

Rug canvas   Aida   Hardanger   Linen/cotton   Evenweave cotton

Silk thread

Machine threads

surface embroidery such as crewel and laid work.

Tapestry wool is a 4-ply twisted yarn, while crewel wool is 2-ply and can be used singly or several strands at a time. 3-stranded Persian wool is loosely twisted.

In addition to cotton and wool threads, *linen* and *silk* are available in specialist shops – linen has a dull, slightly rough surface in contrast to the beautiful lustre of silk.

Machine threads include ordinary sewing cotton and polyester as well as thicker buttonhole twist. In recent years the range of machine embroidery threads has been vastly extended to include metallic-finish and shaded varieties.

Metal threads come in gold, silver, copper and aluminium, ranging in type from fine tambour threads suitable for stitching to thicker cords and braids which have to be couched. Nowadays many people use synthetic threads for metal thread embroidery.

Fabrics
When choosing fabrics, the practical aspect of the project should be considered as well as the colour and texture. Wallhangings and embroidered panels present few practical barriers, whereas garments and household items need a fabric which can be cleaned or washed. For all decorative items, the texture and colour of the background fabric will make a visual impact together with the other materials used.

In addition, it is essential to choose fabrics which are suitable for the particular embroidery technique. Embroidery fabrics are usually cotton or linen, which may be closely woven for surface embroidery and cutwork techniques. Evenweave fabrics, which are always used for counted thread work, are woven, with from 12 to 32 threads per 2.5 cm (1 in). Some, such as Aida and Hardanger fabrics, are constructed with a double-thread weave.

Dress and furnishing fabrics in both natural and synthetic fibres are available in a wide range of textures and patterns. These may be incorporated in appliqué projects or used as backgrounds.

For needlepoint embroidery, there are two main types of woven canvas, those with single or double threads. Both are available in various widths and gauges (or threads per inch. Single (or mono) canvas comes in gauges ranging from 10 to 24 threads per 2.5 cm (1 in) and is more adaptable for stitching a variety of stitches. Double (or Penelope) canvas is mainly used for tramming or for fine details. Rug canvas in gauges 3 to 7 is suitable for large-scale work, and a recent innovation in moulded plastic is used for rigid articles such as boxes and tablemats.

There are a number of subsidiary types of fabrics which are used by embroiderers to support or pad their work.

Wadding is usually made of synthetic fibres, but

sometimes of silk or cotton. Its main use is for quilting (page 101) or for padding and stuffing three-dimensional shapes. Felt can also act as a firm padding or as an insertion in types of appliqué.

Non-woven iron-on or sew-in interfacings used by dressmakers are also suitable for stiffening fabrics for appliqué or for backing finished wallhangings; bonding web is extremely useful for fusing fabrics together.

Dissolvable fabrics used for making lacy effects and constructions by machine come in either hot- or cold-water types (see pages 86–7).

Other equipment
Two pairs of sharp scissors are needed for embroidery – a large pair for cutting out fabric and a small pair for trimming threads and cutting intricate pieces or holes.

Pinking shears are useful for cutting decorative edges. A stiletto, often found in old workboxes, is used for

making eyelets in broderie anglaise.

Using a thimble is largely a matter of personal choice, but will prevent sore fingers when quilting or working in leather. A block of beeswax is useful for techniques such as quilting and metal thread embroidery. The thread is drawn through it, preventing it becoming twisted and helping to give it strength.

Design materials
Most of the equipment needed for designing embroidery is readily at hand. A sketchbook, pencils and some coloured crayons or felt tips are all that are needed for your initial attempts.

If you prefer to use paint, watercolour, poster and gouache are the most useful. Different types of paper, including tracing and graph paper, are required for some methods, while coloured and textured papers and card are good for stencils or for trying out bold ideas. Paper scissors, a craft knife and metal ruler are useful implements when working with paper or card. Fabric and paper adhesives, masking tape and geometry instruments can all be purchased as and when the need arises.

Transferring designs
There are a number of ways of transferring and marking the design on to the background fabric. The method and the type of marker depends on the technique chosen, the fabric and the intricacy of the design. In every case the design should be very lightly marked so that it will not show when the embroidery is complete. Fabric markers include dressmakers' chalk and pencils, water-soluble and air-soluble pens, transfer and permanent pens.

Direct tracing is probably the simplest method for transparent materials. If the fabric is opaque, it can be taped to a window (or a light box) with the design beneath it.

Dressmakers' carbon comes in several colours and works in the same way as ordinary carbon paper.

Pricking and pouncing is one of the oldest methods and is suitable for repeat motifs as only one tracing needs to be made.

Tracing and tacking is best for bold designs. A version of this method is used in machine quilting when the outline of the design is stitched directly through the tracing paper.

Preparation of fabric

If the finished embroidery is to be washed, make sure that the fabric is pre-shrunk or wash it before embarking on the project.

Leave at least 5 cm (2 in) extra fabric around the design to allow room for adjustments, framing or mounting.

Positioning the design

The tracing of the design can often be positioned by eye, but for more precise placing, find the centre of the tracing by folding it into quarters and mark this point, do the same with the fabric and align both marks.

Direct tracing

Outline the original drawing or tracing in black felt tip pen. For fine or transparent fabrics,

tape the tracing to your work surface then tape the fabric in position on top. Trace the design with your chosen marker.

Dressmakers' carbon

Tape the fabric to the work surface. Tape the traced design in position on top with dressmakers' carbon, coloured side down, between the fabric and the tracing. Using a ballpoint pen, draw over the marked lines, pressing firmly.

Pricking and pouncing

Trace the design and turn it over to the reverse side. Place this on a soft surface, such as a piece of felt or a towel. Use a medium-sized needle to prick holes close together along the

marked lines. Position the tracing right side up on the fabric and tape it in place.

Make a pouncing pad by rolling up a small rectangle of felt, holding it together by tying a length of cotton round it. Dip the end of this into a powder made from crushed dressmakers' chalk and charcoal. Rub the powder through the holes in the tracing paper with a circular movement. Remove the tracing and go over the dotted line lightly with your chosen marker.

Tracing and tacking

Trace the design and pin the tracing in position on the fabric. Begin the tacking with a knot and a back stitch and work small running stitches

along the lines through both the paper and the fabric. Fasten off securely.

Gently tear away the tracing paper to leave the tacked line, which may either be covered with the embroidery or removed as the work progresses.

Frames

For the majority of embroidery techniques, the best results are achieved if the work is mounted in a frame. It will remain clean and uncrumpled, and the tension of the stitches will be even. Whichever type of frame is used, the fabric should first be ironed, backed if necessary and the design marked ready for stitching. Care should be taken that the fabric is not distorted in any way but stretched with the warp and weft running at right angles to one another.

Ring (or hoop frames) in wood or metal are available in various sizes and are suitable for small embroidery projects provided the whole of the design will fit within the bounds of the frame. It is not advisable to relocate the frame to another part of the design, as this may cause damage to previously worked areas.

Stretcher frames consist of four lengths of soft wood, with mitred corners, to which the embroidery is fastened with drawing pins.

Tapestry (or slate) frames come in various types. The most satisfactory are those made up of two rollers each with a tape attached to which the canvas or embroidery background fabric is stitched. The rollers are held apart with side battens which have split pins or pegs to adjust the size.

Ring (or hoop) frames

The inner ring may be bound diagonally with bias binding

to protect fine or delicate fabrics. This also provides a better grip for free machine embroidery.

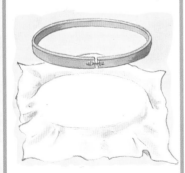

Adjust the screw of the outer ring so that it fits loosely over the inner ring. Place the fabric

over the inner ring. Press the outer ring down over the fabric and the inner ring, making sure the fabric is straight, taut and the area to be worked is in the centre of the ring. Tighten the screw to secure the fabric.

Stretcher frames

Mark the centre of each side of the frame and make corresponding marks on the fabric. Then, starting at the top edge, align the centre marks and secure with a drawing pin. Continue pinning at 12-mm (½-in) intervals, working

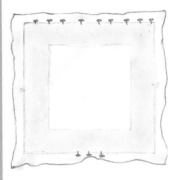

towards the sides. Turn the frame and fasten the bottom edge in a similar way, stretching the fabric taut.

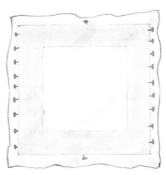

To complete the other two sides, pin the centre points and continue towards the ends,

pinning first one side and then the other to tension the fabric evenly.

Tapestry (or slate) frames

Mark the centre point of the fabric and fold a 12-mm (½-in) hem to the wrong side along the top and bottom edges, and a 2.5 cm (1 in) hem along the sides. Cut two lengths of string at least 45 cm (18 in) longer than the side battens.

Place these inside the side hems and machine stitch near the edge to form a casing over each string.

With wrong sides together, align the centre points on the top and bottom edges with the centre markings on the roller tape. Pin the fabric along the tape and overcast them together with strong, doubled

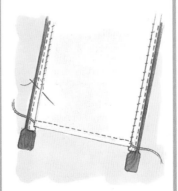

thread, starting in the centre and working towards the edges.

Insert the side battens and secure them with the split pins or pegs so that the fabric is taut. Tie the ends of the strings to the rollers. Lace the sides of the fabric to the side battens using string, threaded in a large-eyed needle. Pull the string to tighten the fabric and tie the ends around the batten ends.

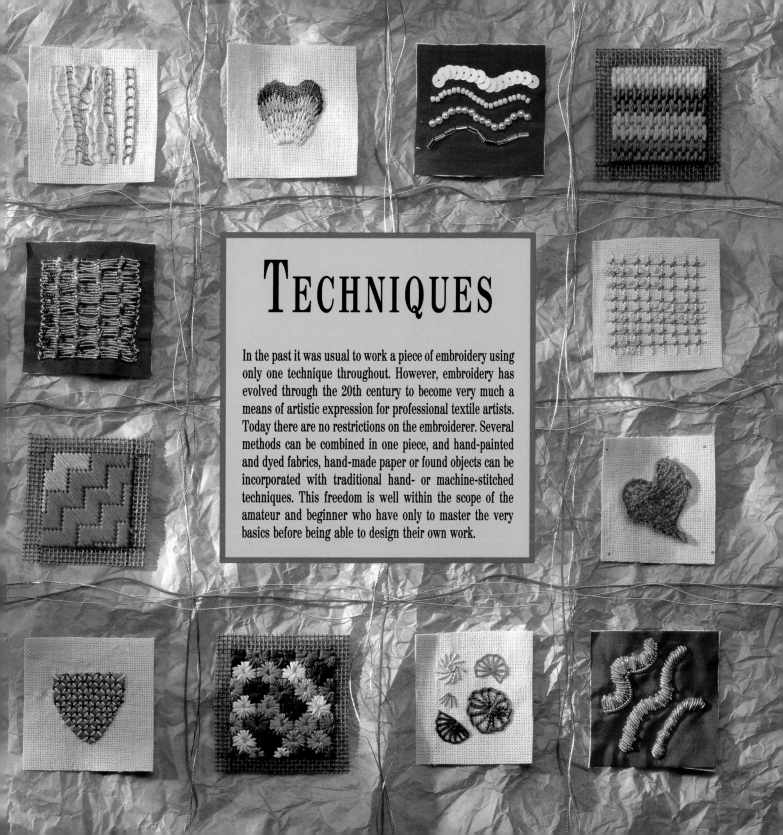

TECHNIQUES

In the past it was usual to work a piece of embroidery using only one technique throughout. However, embroidery has evolved through the 20th century to become very much a means of artistic expression for professional textile artists. Today there are no restrictions on the embroiderer. Several methods can be combined in one piece, and hand-painted and dyed fabrics, hand-made paper or found objects can be incorporated with traditional hand- or machine-stitched techniques. This freedom is well within the scope of the amateur and beginner who have only to master the very basics before being able to design their own work.

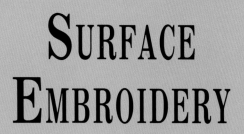

SURFACE EMBROIDERY

LINE STITCHES • COUCHING

CHAIN STITCHES

BAND AND BORDER STITCHES

CRETAN AND FEATHER STITCH

SATIN STITCHES

LONG AND SHORT STITCH

RAISED STITCHES • ROUND MOTIFS

ISOLATED STITCHES

CREWEL WORK • INSERTION STITCHES

LAIDWORK

A repertoire of surface stitches is the main element of almost every type of embroidery. Knowing a collection of basic stitches plus a few more unusual ones will enable you to create different effects and work many techniques.

Surface embroidery is sometimes known as free-style stitchery because the stitches are worked independently of the weave of the background fabric, and unlike counted thread embroidery, can be made in any direction and in an infinite variety of yarns.

Stitches can be grouped in a number of ways, to make lines, form circles or create wide bands of pattern. Some are used as small isolated elements, sprinkled across the surface, while others may fill a space more solidly.

However, even though a stitch falls into a certain category when used conventionally, it can usually be adapted or modified to produce a different effect. When the working of a stitch has been mastered, it is a good idea to experiment by altering the scale and direction, by working haphazardly or using varying thicknesses and different types of yarn. Some stitches can be over-lapped, while others can be worked in twists, spirals and circular motifs. This type of experimentation will produce ideas for subjects or elements in a design, and you will find inspiration from the shapes, patterns and textures which you create with fabric and thread.

Fabrics

Although the traditional fabric used for surface embroidery is either linen or cotton, today's embroiderers are happy to use any background fabric which suits their purpose. For practical articles such as table linen, consideration naturally needs to be given to its uses. But embroidered pictures, panels and wallhangings present few barriers and the background may be chosen mainly for its colour and texture. For this type of work the background fabric can be supported on a backing fabric and the embroidery stitched through both layers. For the best results it is preferable to mount the work in a frame.

Threads

Threads for surface embroidery may include the full range of embroidery threads (page 8) and others such as knitting wools, crochet cottons and even string, tapes and ribbons (page 118). In general terms the weight and thickness of the thread should be matched to that of the fabric, but it is often possible to disregard this rule for decorative effect. A variety of yarns can be used for unusual and creative work provided you can pull the thread through the fabric without distortion.

Needles

Select embroidery needles suitable to the thickness of the yarn, or chenille needles, which have a larger hole for taking thicker threads.

LINE STITCHES

Some of the most useful stitches are those which make thin lines naturally – such as running, stem, chain and couching. They can be used for defining or outlining shapes as well as for depicting stems of flowers, blades of grass or branches of trees; and worked in flowing lines they will give movement to a design. Rows of line stitches can also be worked close together to fill an area more solidly.

Running stitch, the simplest of all, makes a broken line. This stitch is often seen in hand quilting, but is also useful as a basis for ornamentation combined with whipping and interlacing.

Back stitch forms a continuous thin line similar to machine stitching, while *stem stitch* produces rope-like lines which can vary in thickness depending on the angle at which the needle is inserted.

Running stitch

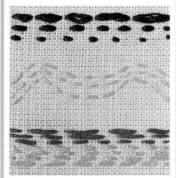

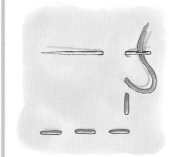

Working from right to left, bring the needle in and out of the fabric at regular intervals, making evenly spaced stitches. Running stitch can be varied by working stitches of different lengths and with irregular spaces. Solid rows of stitching can be built up to give a flat texture.

Whipped running stitch

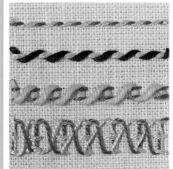

Work a row of evenly spaced running stitches. Starting with a new thread in a tapestry needle, bring the needle up alongside the first stitch and take it through the next stitch but not through the fabric. Repeat. Variations can be made by using a contrasting thread for whipping or by altering the length and spacing of the running stitches. Multiple rows of running stitch can also be whipped.

Interlaced running stitch

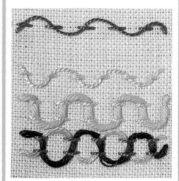

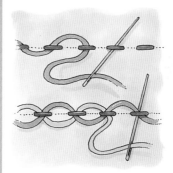

Work a row of evenly spaced running stitches. Using a tapestry needle and another thread, take the needle alternately up and down through the stitches but not through the fabric. A third thread can be interlaced similarly from the reverse direction. Multiple rows of running stitches can also be interlaced.

Back stitch

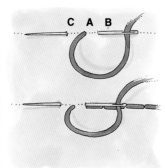

Bring the needle up at A, a short distance from the starting point (B), then take it down at the starting point and bring it out ahead of A at C. This makes a smooth, continuous row of stitching suitable for outlines and for blackwork and Italian quilting.

Pekinese stitch

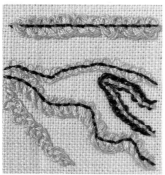

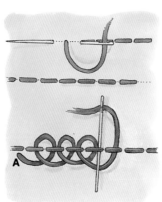

Work a line of back stitch. Using a tapestry needle, bring the needle out at A and take it up through the next but one back stitch (but not through the fabric) and back down through the previous back stitch to form a circular loop. The tension may be loose or tight, but should be kept even.

Stem stitch

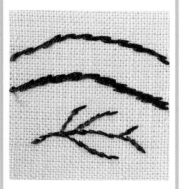

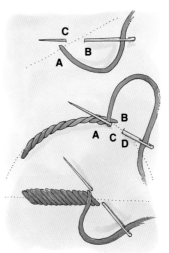

Working from left to right, bring the needle up at A, take it down at B along the stitching line and bring it up at C halfway between A and B. For the second stitch insert the needle at D. While working, keep the thread either above the stitching line or below.

The thickness of stem stitch can be varied by taking the stitch diagonally across the stitching line.

Split stitch

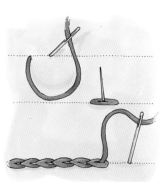

This is worked in a similar way to stem stitch, but the needle is brought up halfway through the previous stitch, splitting the thread.

Split stitch produces a thin line which is useful for filling spaces, or as a preparatory outline stitch for satin or long and short stitch.

COUCHING

Couched threads are those which are laid on the surface and secured by means of a series of small stitches made over them, usually worked at regular intervals.

Couching, used for metal thread work and for attaching yarns which are too thick or textured to go through the background, is a versatile method; the type of threads and couching stitches can be varied to produce many different effects. It is essential to work couching on fabric which is tautly framed.

Couching

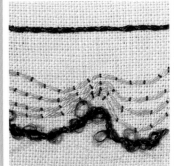

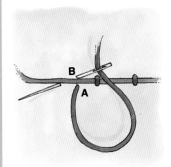

Bring out the thread to be couched at the start of the stitching line, remove the needle and use your non-stitching hand to hold the thread taut on the fabric. Bring the couching thread through a little way along the stitching line at A and take a small vertical stitch over the laid thread to B. Repeat to the end of the stitching line and fasten off. Rethread the couched thread, take it through to the back of the work and fasten off. If the couched thread is very thick, pull it through with pliers and secure with a few stitches in a fine thread.

Pendant couching

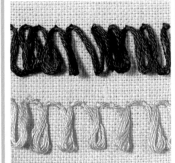

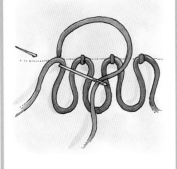

Pendant couching is worked in a similar way to couching except that the couching stitches are worked fairly close together and the laid thread is left loose to form a loop.

Trailing

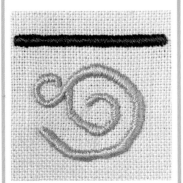

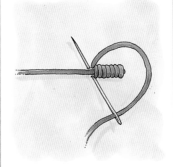

In this form of couching the laid thread is completely covered by couching stitches worked close together and taking up as little of the background fabric as possible so that a raised cord is produced.

CHAIN STITCHES

Chain stitch and its variations are all based on bringing the working thread through the loop to produce a slightly raised line. Tension is important in order to retain the chain effect, but simple *chain stitch* can be worked evenly or with loops of different sizes. *Whipped chain* gives a raised rope-like line, while *open chain,* as its name implies, recreates a wide open line.

Rosette chain has a pretty textured braid effect and can also be stitched in circular formation to produce flower shapes (page 29).

Twisted chain is worked in a similar way to chain stitch, except that the needle is inserted to the side of the loop. If twisted chain is embroidered very small with a longer stitch between the loops, it produces *coral stitch.*

Double knot stitch is similar in effect to coral stitch but with heavier knots.

Chain stitch

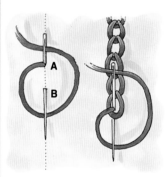

Work this stitch towards you from top to bottom. Bring the needle up at A and insert it again into the same hole, leaving a loop. Bring the needle up through the loop on the stitching line at B. Repeat. To finish, take a vertical stitch to secure the loop.

Whipped chain stitch

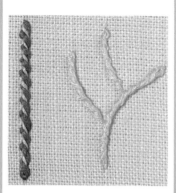

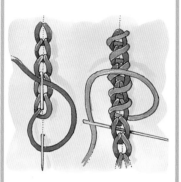

Work a row of chain stitch. Then, using a toning or contrasting thread in a tapestry needle, bring the needle up alongside the first stitch and take it under the loop but not through the fabric. Repeat through the next stitch.

Open chain stitch

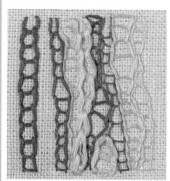

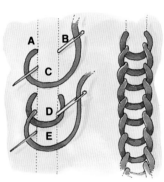

This is worked in a similar way to chain stitch, but in a wider form. Bring the needle up at A, insert it at B, leaving a loop, and bring it out at C, leaving the thread loose. Take the needle down at D inside the loop and bring it out again at E. Repeat. To finish take two vertical stitches to secure the final loop.

Twisted chain stitch

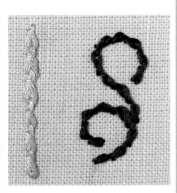

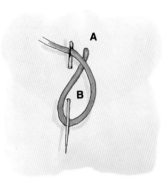

Worked in a similar way to chain stitch except that the needle is inserted outside the loop to the left of A and brought through the loop at B, forming the twist.

Repeat the process as above.

Coral stitch

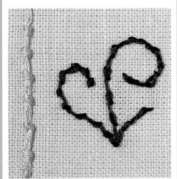

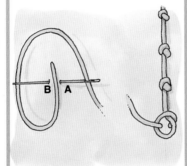

Worked in a similar way to twisted chain stitch except that the needle is taken horizontally across the stitching line, from A, emerging through the loop at B to form a small knot. Repeat a short distance away from the first knot.

Rosette chain

Work this stitch from right to left. Begin with a single twisted chain stitch. Slip the needle up through the first part of the stitch but not through the fabric. Repeat.

Double knot stitch

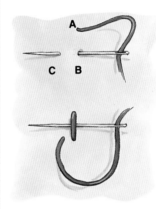

Bring the needle up at A and take up a small amount of fabric across the stitching line from B to C. Slip the needle under the vertical stitch and pull the thread tight.

Work a chain stitch through the vertical stitch but not through the fabric.

19

BAND & BORDER STITCHES

When worked conventionally this group of stitches produces wide borders or bands of texture. All the stitches, however, can be adapted and worked freely to produce some of the most interesting effects in the embroiderer's repertoire.

Buttonhole, also known as blanket stitch, is extremely versatile – it can be used for edgings as in cutwork (page 111) and appliqué (page 88), or as a decorative stitch in its own right, when it can be worked evenly or at random to produce many different effects. *Buttonhole wheels* are made by stitching in a circle (page 29).

Herringbone stitch can be embroidered in a very regular fashion with even spaces which may be apart or very close together. It can also serve as a basis for embellishment by interlacing or threading as in *threaded herringbone*.

Buttonhole stitch

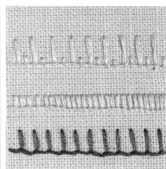

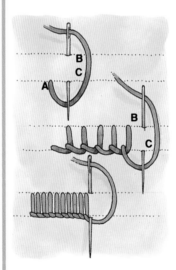

Bring the needle out at A, insert it at B above the stitching line and bring it out again at C through the loop. Repeat, starting again at B. To finish, secure with a small stitch to hold the loop.

Up-and-down buttonhole

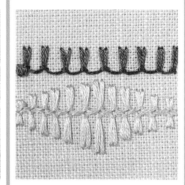

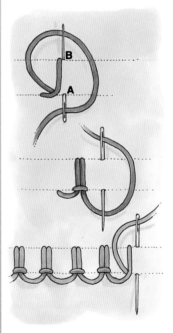

Work a single buttonhole stitch. Insert the needle at A and bring it out at B alongside the first stitch and through the loop. Repeat and finish as for buttonhole stitch.

Herringbone stitch

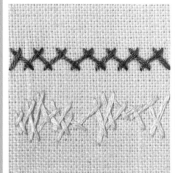

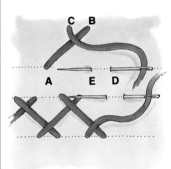

Working from left to right, bring the needle out at A on the lower stitching line and take a diagonal stitch to B. Bring the needle out at C a short distance to left of B and take a diagonal stitch in the other direction to D. Bring the needle out at E to repeat.

Close herringbone stitch

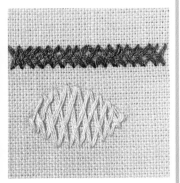

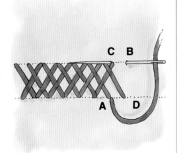

This is worked in a similar way to herringbone stitch but close together, with the stitches touching one another.

Threaded herringbone stitch

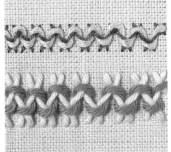

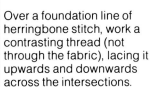

Over a foundation line of herringbone stitch, work a contrasting thread (not through the fabric), lacing it upwards and downwards across the intersections.

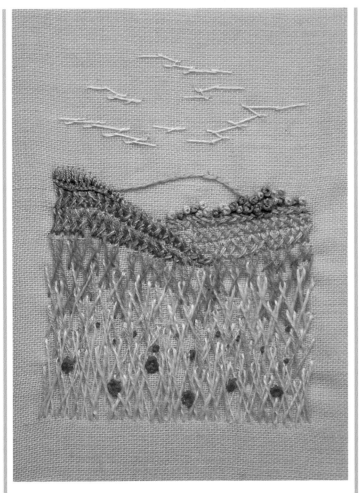

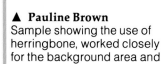

▲ **Pauline Brown**
Sample showing the use of herringbone, worked closely for the background area and freely for the cornfield.

CRETAN AND FEATHER STITCH

Evenly worked in a similar way to herringbone stitch, *open Cretan stitch* forms a zigzag line, but when stitched freely in over-lapping formation, interesting textures can be built up. It is often used for depicting grasses, or if worked vertically is useful for shadows or water effects.

Closed Cretan is stitched in a similar way, but more fabric is picked up for each stitch, which produces a central plait. Worked as a filling stitch it is especially good for leaves and other motifs requiring a ridge down the centre.

The whole range of *feather stitches*, particularly *closed feather*, is suitable for decorative borders. *Single* and *double feather* can be stitched haphazardly to create vegetation such as trees and bushes.

Open Cretan stitch

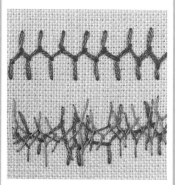

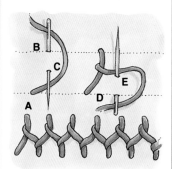

Bring the needle up at A on the lower stitching line. Insert it at B above and slightly to the right and bring it out directly below at C, keeping the thread to the right. Then insert the needle at D and bring it up at E, still keeping the thread to the right.

Closed Cretan stitch

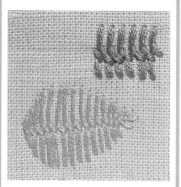

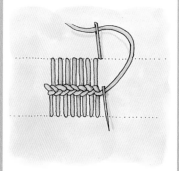

This is worked in a similar way to open Cretan, but with the stitches worked closer together to cover the fabric.

▼ Daphne Ashby
Sheep
This piece demonstrates the free use of Cretan stitch. Different effects can be achieved by taking up more or less amounts of fabric and by varying the distances between each stitch. You can also overlap rows of stitches to build up a textured surface.

Feather stitch

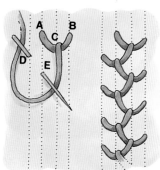

Bring the needle up at A, insert it at B and, keeping the thread towards you, bring it up at C through the loop. Repeat the stitch below and to the left, at D and E, then work another to the right. Repeat.

Double feather stitch

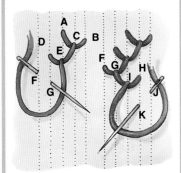

This is stitched in a similar way to single, but two stitches are worked to the right and left alternately. This stitch can be varied by altering the distances between stitches and the angle at which they are worked.

Closed feather stitch

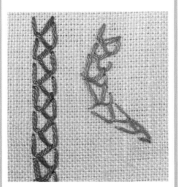

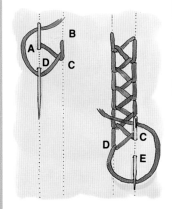

The formation of this variation is similar to single feather stitch. Bring the needle up at A, insert it at B and bring it up at C through the loop. Insert the needle just below A, bring it up at D, insert it just below C, and bring it out at E.

▲ **Pauline Brown**
Feather stitch is ideal for depicting the delicate tracery of this willow.

SATIN STITCHES

Satin stitch is especially beautiful when it is worked in pure silk floss or other threads which reflect the light to give the characteristic smooth, shiny look.

Although at first sight it seems quite easy, it is actually one of the most difficult stitches to work well: the individual stitches need to be embroidered exactly parallel to one another with the threads lying smoothly. In order to preserve a well-defined shape, satin stitch should be embroidered at an angle wherever possible. An outline of split stitch (page 16) with the satin stitch worked on top will help to keep the edge smooth.

The length of stitches should be limited as they may become unwieldy and liable to snag; large areas should be broken up into smaller sections.

Padded satin gives a raised effect suitable for a small area, such as the centre of a flower, with a second layer of satin stitch worked over the first row.

Satin stitch

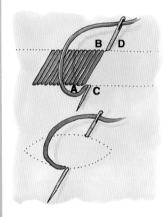

Bring the needle up at A on one edge of the shape to be covered, and insert it at B, diagonally across on the opposite edge. Bring the needle up at C, immediately next to A, and insert it at D.

Padded satin stitch

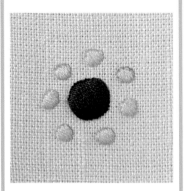

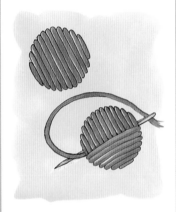

Fill the area with satin stitch and then work a second layer on top at right angles to the first. For a more raised effect a third layer can be stitched.

Voiding

This is a characteristic of Chinese embroidery, in which areas of satin stitch, often worked on a dark background, are stitched with a narrow but clearly defined space between.

Encroaching satin stitch

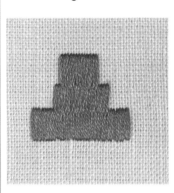

This is a useful method for filling an area, with subsequent rows worked slightly into the previous ones, producing an interlocked woven effect.

◀ **Nancy Martin**
An unusual treatment with solidly worked satin stitch.

LONG AND SHORT STITCH

Long and short stitch is most often used for shading motifs such as petals and leaves, and can create very realistic effects. Practice is required to perfect a smooth gradation both of stitching and colour.

This stitch is worked in a similar way to satin, but the first row has stitches of unequal length, with subsequent rows interlocking. A rectangular area is relatively simple to cover in this way, but with shapes which diminish in size, such as petals, it is trickier, as the number and size of the stitches will gradually lessen.

Long and short stitch

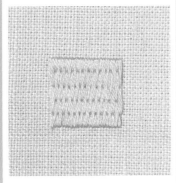

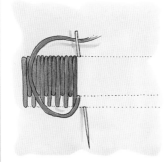

1 For a rectangular shape, begin with a row of long and short vertical stitches worked alternately.

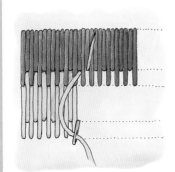

2 The second and subsequent rows are made with stitches of equal length fitting into the spaces.

Shaping and shading

1 Define the outside edge of a shape such as a petal with the first row of long and short stitch in a dark colour. Begin at the centre at A and work to the right before returning to the centre and working to the left. The stitches should radiate towards the centre of the flower.

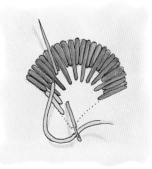

2 For subsequent rows in gradually changing shades, work equal length stitches between. It is necessary to eliminate some stitches as the shape dictates.

RAISED STITCHES

The textural effect of raised embroidery stitches can quite literally bring another dimension to creative work.

Raised chain and *stem bands* are both worked on a "ladder" of straight stitches which may be of even or uneven width and spaced uniformly or randomly. The chain and stem stitches are then worked on the ladder foundation, either in single or multiple rows. Thick or textured threads can be used if desired as they only have to be inserted through the background fabric at the start and the finish.

Buttonhole loops look best when massed together, while *raised herringbone* is usually worked as an individual motif or grouped in a flower or leaf form. *Woven picots* were originally made as a minute triangular edging stitch, but nowadays are often used to depict leaves.

Raised chain band

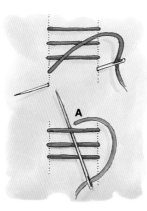

1 Make a series of evenly spaced horizontal straight stitches. Using a contrasting thread in a tapestry needle, bring the needle up at A just above the centre of the first stitch.

Bring the needle over and up under the first stitch to the left (not through the fabric).

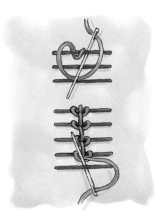

2 Then bring the needle down under the first stitch to the right of the working thread, and pull through the loop. Repeat, keeping the tension even.

Raised stem band

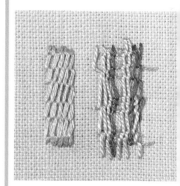

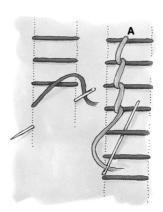

Work a narrow ladder of stitches as for raised chain band. Bring the needle out at A above the first horizontal stitch.

Then bring the needle over and up under the first stitch to the right (as for conventional stem stitch but not through the fabric). Repeat. For best effect, work several rows.

Buttonhole loops

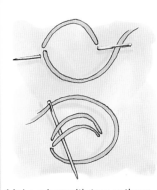

Make a bar with two or three loose straight stitches one on top of the other.

Then work a series of buttonhole stitches (page 20) to cover the foundation bar (but not through the fabric). Depending on the length and looseness of the bar, different effects can be created.

Raised herringbone stitch

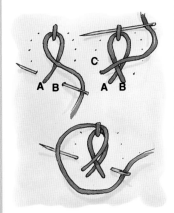

Make a small vertical straight stitch. Bring the needle up at A below and to the left of this, take it through the straight stitch (but not through the fabric) and insert it at B to the right on a level with A. Bring the needle out at C, just above A and repeat the stitch three or four times to produce a leaf shape.

Woven picots

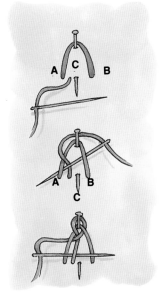

1 Insert pin to take up as much fabric as the finished size of the picot. Bring the needle out at A to the left of the pin and take the thread round the top of the pin and insert the needle at B. Bring the needle out again at C, and take the thread round the top of the pin as before. Begin weaving on this foundation of three threads, taking the needle under, over and under on the first run. Then weave from left to right over, under and over.

2 Continue until the base of the picot is reached. Maintain a loose tension so that the triangular form of the picot is preserved.

ROUND MOTIFS

Circular stitches are ideal for motifs such as flowers, berries or wheels. Although many stitches, such as chain or satin stitch, can of course be worked to form a round shape, there are a number which naturally produce circular motifs. *Woven wheels* and *woven spider's webs* are both embroidered on a foundation of straight stitches radiating from a central point, with woven wheels having a smooth texture and spider's webs being more knobbly.

Raised cup is more unusual. This is worked on a base of back stitch in a type of twisted buttonhole stitch, producing a small raised circular outline.

Rosette chain (page 19) can be stitched in a ring to create a pretty flower shape, and *buttonhole stitch* (page 20), well-known for its versatility, can be embroidered with the loop either at the centre of the circle or on the outer edge.

Woven wheels

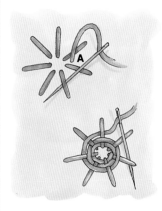

Work a circle of seven straight stitches radiating from a central point. Using a tapestry needle and a long thread, bring the needle up at A near the centre of the circle. Take the needle alternately under and over the straight stitches until the circle is filled.

Woven spider's webs

Make a foundation circle of any number of straight stitches as for woven wheels. Bring the needle up at A near the centre of the circle. Take the needle under two radiating stitches (but not through the fabric), back over the second thread and then under both it and the next one. Proceed with this back stitch movement (page 16) around the circle, gradually loosening the tension until the radiating stitches are covered.

Variations on woven wheels and spider's webs
The number and length of the base threads can be altered, and these can be left partly uncovered if desired. Colours and textures can also be varied to provide added interest.

Raised cup stitch

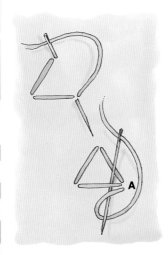

Work a foundation of three back stitches (page 16) in triangular formation. Bring the needle up at A just outside the triangle. Work a series of twisted buttonhole stitches from right to left on the back stitch foundation (but not through the fabric) until a tiny raised circle is achieved.

Rosette chain wheel

Work a series of rosette chain stitches (page 19) to form a circular motif.

Buttonhole wheels

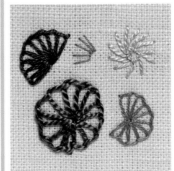

Working with the loop on the outside, stitch a series of buttonhole stitches (page 20) to form a circle. Half and quarter circles can also be created. For a spiky effect, work with the loop at the centre of the circle. The length of the stitches can also be varied.

▼ **Pauline Brown**
Woven and rosette chain wheels form the flower heads, and the leaves are worked in buttonhole stitch.

ISOLATED STITCHES

There are a number of detached stitches which can be used individually as tiny motifs, or scattered across an area to make patterns or alter the tone of the background. If massed together, these stitches will create texture, or when grouped can form decorative motifs.

French and *bullion knots* are often used for the centres of flowers, and they can both be worked with "tails", which can simulate stamens or tiny trees. Bullion knots can be varied by stitching them on a loose thread, giving an effect similar to buttonhole loops (page 27).

Detached chain stitch, also known as daisy stitch or lazy daisy, is usually embroidered in a flower shape, while *wheatear* and *fern stitch* are both useful additions for floral subjects.

Fly stitch seems at first sight to be very ordinary but in fact is extremely versatile as the length of the "tail" and the appearance can be varied to produce different shapes.

French knots

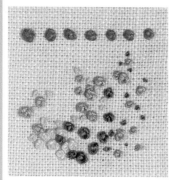

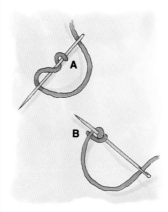

Bring the needle out at A, hold the thread taut between the forefinger and thumb of your non-working hand and twist the needle round the thread twice. Insert the needle halfway at B, pull the twist down the needle so that it lies on the fabric, then push the needle through to the back of the work.

Variations
Both French knots and bullion knots can be worked with tails. In each case, after forming the knot, insert the needle a short distance away. Bullion loops can be made by inserting the needle a tiny distance away from the starting point and winding the thread round the needle many times.

Bullion knots

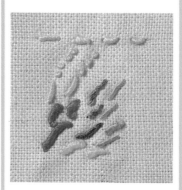

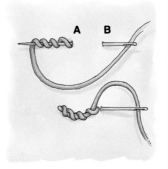

Bring the needle out at A. Insert it the required length of the stitch at B, bringing it halfway out again at A. Twist the thread round the needle about six times, then hold the twist with your thumb, and pull the needle and thread through both the fabric and the twist. Pull the needle and thread back towards B and insert the needle at B.

Detached chain stitch

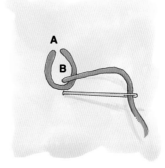

Bring the needle up at A and insert it again into the same hole, leaving a loop. Bring it up through the loop on the stitching line at B. To finish take a vertical stitch to secure the loop. This last stitch can be tiny or quite long.

Wheatear stitch

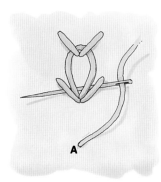

Make two small straight stitches in the form of a V. Bring the needle out at A a short distance below the V, pass it through the straight stitches (but not through the fabric) and insert it again at A. This can also be used as a continuous decorative line stitch.

Fern stitch

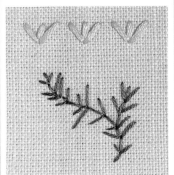

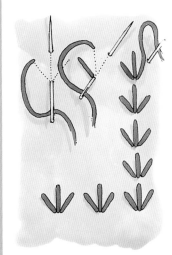

Make three small straight stitches all radiating from the central hole. This can also be used as a continuous line stitch.

Fly stitch

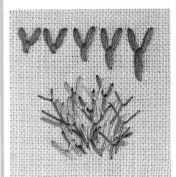

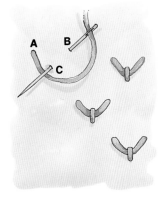

Worked in a similar way to detached chain, except that the needle is brought up at A, inserted a small distance away at B, and brought up again through the loop at C. The fastening stitch can be long or short.

Variations
Detached chain can be doubled in size by working another around the first, while wheatear can be thickened with an extra loop stitched through the straight stitches. Fly stitch and detached chain can both be worked with long or short tails.

▲ **Pauline Brown**
Fly stitch in raffia and stranded cotton forms a stylized tree.

INSERTION STITCHES

Although insertion stitches are seldom now seen in their traditional role – as a decorative means of joining sections of garments together – they are an interesting group of stitches and can be used inventively on wallhangings and embroidered panels to hold areas of the design or different fabrics together.

The folded-back hems of the fabrics must first be joined onto a firm backing such as strong paper, and the insertion stitches are then worked on the surface across the gap. Yarns such as coton à broder, pearl cotton or crochet cotton are the most suitable as the threads will not separate.

Faggoting, or twisted insertion, is the most familiar stitch, producing a zigzag effect, as does *knotted insertion*. An easy type of insertion can be made with groups of *buttonhole stitch* (page 20) worked alternately on the upper and lower edges of the fabric.

Preparation for insertion stitches

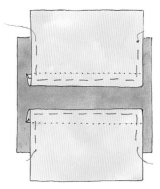

The edges of two pieces of fabric between which the insertion stitch is to be worked must first be folded over and hemmed in place. To preserve good tension and evenness of stitch, tack them on a base of firm brown paper, leaving a space of from 6 mm (¼ in) to 2.5 cm (1 in) according to the width of the required insertion stitch.

Faggoting

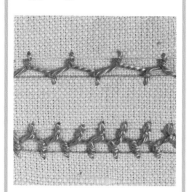

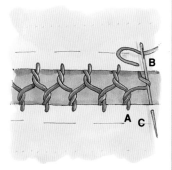

Working from left to right, bring the needle up at A, take it across the space and up again at B. From the right. pass the needle under and over the thread and bring it up again at C. Repeat.

Buttonhole insertion stitch

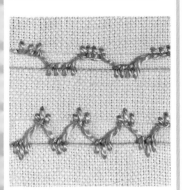

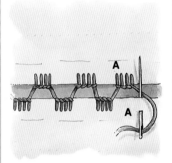

Bring the needle out at A and work three or four buttonhole stitches over the folded edge of the fabric. Take the thread diagonally across the space to the opposite folded edge and work another set of buttonhole stitches. Repeat. The effect of this stitch can be varied by altering the height of the buttonhole stitches or leaving more or less space between them.

Knotted insertion stitch

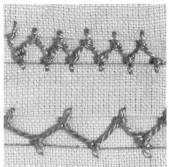

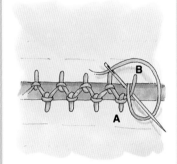

The knotted stitch is worked alternately from edge to edge. Bring the needle up from the back of the fabric at A and insert it further along to the right at B, making a diagonal stitch and keeping the thread to the right; then make a buttonhole stitch loop to secure the diagonal thread. Take the thread diagonally across to the other edge and repeat the knotted stitch on the other edge.

▶ **Pauline Brown**
An insertion stitch sampler applied to backgrounds of different colours.

CREWEL WORK

Crewel work, traditionally worked in fine "crewel" wools on linen, is one of the earliest forms of English surface stitchery. It was very popular in 17th-century England – it is sometimes known as Jacobean embroidery – and was also used by William Morris and his followers in the late 19th century.

▲ **Joanne Dixey**
Traditional-style Jacobean crewel work embroidery.

Fabrics
Natural linen or linen crash are the traditional fabrics, but other materials with weaves suitable to take fine wool threads can also be used. The fabric should be framed to accommodate the intricate filling stitches.

Threads
Fine tapestry or crewel wool are most often used, but other yarns may be chosen for a contemporary approach.

Needles
Crewel (or embroidery) needles are the most satisfactory.

Designs
Crewel work is characterized by its linear form combined with areas such as leaves and flowers filled with decorative stitches. Transfer the design by direct tracing (page 10), transfer pen or dressmakers' carbon paper.

Stitches
Crewel work incorporates many of the most familiar embroidery stitches, but there are several which are particular to this technique, including *trellis* and *honeycomb filling* both of which make decorative fillings. *Tête-de-boeuf* is an isolated motif stitch which can be scattered in a pattern, while *battlement couching* produces a three-dimensional effect.

Trellis stitch

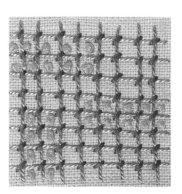

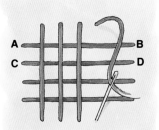
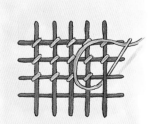

1 Make a row of parallel horizontal straight stitches by bringing the needle up at A, inserting it at B, bringing it up again at C and inserting it at D. Repeat, and then work a similar row on top at right angles to the first.

2 Using a similar or contrasting thread, make small diagonal straight stitches over each inter-section. This stitch can be further elaborated with stitches such as cross, detached chain, French knots etc. in some or all the spaces.

Other stitches for crewel work
Buttonhole stitch (page 20) Fly stitch (page 31)
Chain stitch (page 17) French knots (page 30)
Twisted chain (page 19) Bullion knots (page 30)
Couching (page 17) Laidwork (page 36)
Satin stitch (page 24)
Long and short stitch
  (page 25)

Honeycomb filling stitch

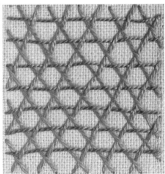

1 Work a series of parallel horizontal straight stitches as for trellis stitch. Stitch a second row of diagonal stitches on top of the first.

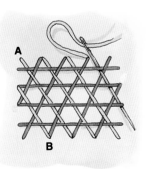

2 For the third layer, bring the needle out at A, and then take it across to B, weaving under and over the first two layers of stitches to achieve the honeycomb effect.

Tête-de-boeuf stitch

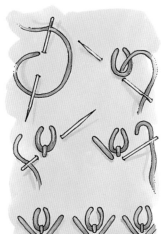

Make a single detached chain stitch (page 31) between two straight stitches set at right angles to one another. This stitch is normally worked in a half-drop formation to form a decorative filling.

Battlement couching

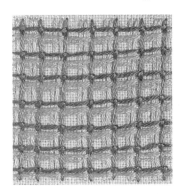

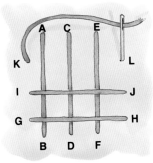

1 To achieve the most effective result, the layers of stitches should be worked in threads which are graded in tone. Make a grid of vertical straight stitches from A to F with horizontal ones crossing them from G to L.

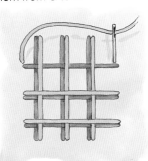

2 Lay another grid of stitches in a different colour, to the right of the vertical stitches and above the horizontal.

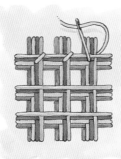

3 Repeat and secure the top grid with small diagonal stitches across the intersections.

LAIDWORK

Notably found in oriental silk embroidery and English crewel work, laidwork consists of a series of couched lines worked side by side to fill a space. Originally developed as an economical method of using precious silk or metal, the laid base threads are secured decoratively in a selection of different patterns.

The laidwork base differs from satin stitch in that the underneath stitches do not cover the back of the fabric, but are taken along the edge of the shape to be stitched. *Romanian* and *Bokhara couching* are similarly worked, by laying threads and securing them in one process. For Romanian couching, a stitch is taken across the space and held down with long diagonal stitches on the return journey. As the work progresses the tying stitches are worked to form a textured surface, so that the laid stitches are indistinguishable from those holding them. Bokhara couching is embroidered in a similar way but the tying stitches are shorter and usually form an overall diagonal pattern.

Fabrics
If laidwork stitches are incorporated in a crewel work design (page 34) the natural choice would be linen or linen crash. For a silk embroidery, a more delicate fabric, such as silk or satin mounted on a cotton backing, is more appropriate.

Threads
Crewel wool for crewel designs. Stranded cotton or floss silk for oriental-type embroidery.

Needles
Crewel or embroidery needles of appropriate size.

Laid base

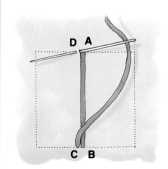

Make a series of straight vertical stitches parallel to one another from A to B and C to D. Care should be taken that the top and bottom edges are even and that the background fabric is covered.

Straight stitch laidwork

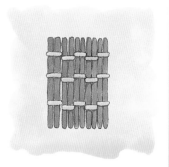

On a laid base, work a series of small straight stitches to hold individual or pairs of laid threads in place to create a surface pattern. These can be stitched in straight lines, brick formation, scallops or diamonds.

Laidwork trellis

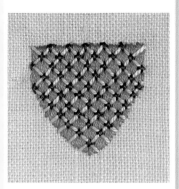

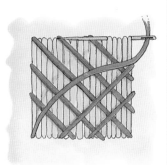

1 Over a laid base, work a grid of diagonal stitches as for trellis stitch (page 34).

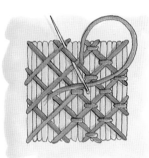

2 Secure these with a small stitch worked at each intersection.

Romanian couching

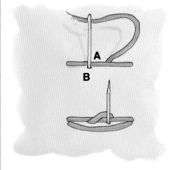

Normally used as a filling stitch, but occasionally as a border. Embroider a straight stitch across the area to be filled, bring the needle up at A and insert it at B, making a long, obliquely slanting stitch to give a woven appearance.

Bokhara couching

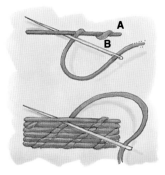

Work a straight stitch as for Romanian couching. For the first tying stitch, bring the needle out at A, make a small diagonal stitch to B, continue with similar diagonal stitches at regular intervals.

▲ **Pamela Rooke**
Laidwork is used here to create the solidity of the robes.

NEEDLEPOINT

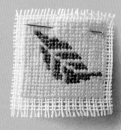

BASIC TECHNIQUE

CROSSED STITCHES

DIAGONAL STITCHES

EYELETS

SQUARE STITCHES

LEAVES AND FLOWERS

TEXTURED STITCHES

BARGELLO EMBROIDERY

FOUR-WAY BARGELLO

Of all embroidery techniques needlepoint is perhaps the most popular. Also known as canvaswork, or tapestry – the latter because it was developed as a stitched imitation of woven tapestry – it has been practised since the 16th century. It achieved widespread use in the 19th century when Berlin woolwork, as it was then known, was stitched for all types of articles from slippers and smoking caps to upholstery on chairs and footstools. This work was done solely in tent (or half cross) stitch, but today's embroiderers prefer to extend the range of stitches and threads to produce a wide variety of raised, patterned and textural effects.

Canvas
Single or double canvas (page 9) can be used depending on the type of stitch, the design and the practical use (if any) to which the needlepoint will be put.

Threads
Tapestry, Persian and crewel wools are most often chosen for needlepoint, but different textures and fibres, such as stranded and pearl cotton, knitting and crochet yarns can add interest to a design. Ribbons and tapes can also be used experimentally. Threads should be chosen to fit with the gauge of the canvas and also with the type of stitch – vertical stitches do not cover the canvas as well as those which are worked diagonally.

Needles
Tapestry needles come in sizes from 13 to 24. Select a size which slips easily between the canvas mesh.

Frames
It is essential to frame needlepoint embroidery, as distortion is likely to occur if the work is stitched in the hand, particularly with diagonal stitches. Rectangular handheld or floorstanding frames are available or you can use a wooden stretcher with the canvas pinned in place. Circular embroidery hoops are not suitable.

Designs
Very many types of design are suitable for translating into needlepoint. The canvas mesh makes it an ideal medium for geometric designs which can be worked out on a line chart (page 39). Pictorial and abstract subjects with areas of the design filled with different stitches are also popular. Although commercially produced kits often have the entire design painted onto the canvas, for more spontaneous and creative work you only need to mark the outlines so that the areas can be freely filled with stitches.

PREPARATION

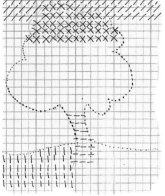

Preparing the canvas
Cut the canvas along the threads and ensure that the corners are square. If a stretcher frame is being used, bind all four edges with masking tape; if working on a slate frame bind the side edges only.

For geometric designs mark the centre of the canvas with vertical and horizontal lines using a waterproof marking pen.

Transferring the design
Outline the main lines of the design with a black felt-tip pen and tape it to your working surface. Position and tape the canvas centrally on top of the design and then trace the design using a waterproof marker. Details can be added as the needlepoint proceeds. For more elaborate designs, the canvas can be painted, using a little paint and a fairly dry brush. Use a waterproof paint such as fabric paint or acrylic.

Following a line chart
On this type of chart, the lines represent the threads of the canvas, with the stitches drawn between or diagonally across the grid. The stitches are then worked vertically, horizontally or diagonally, corresponding to the diagram.

When stitching, always count the number of canvas threads or intersections over which the stitch is worked. Bring the needle up at A and insert it at B and so on.

▶ **Jenifer Murray**
Plus ça change, plus c'est la même chose
Geometric needlepoint design that includes a wide variety of stitches.

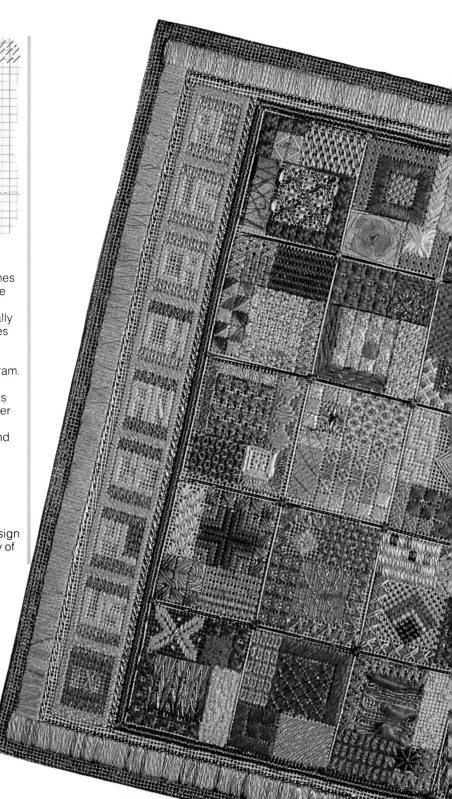

BASIC TECHNIQUE

Working needlepoint in a frame makes it much faster as well as preventing distortion. One hand is used to push the needle into the canvas from above with a stabbing movement, while the other, below the canvas, pulls it through.

Only a short length of thread should be used as the canvas tends to wear the yarn as the stitching proceeds. If possible the needle should come up through an empty hole and go down in one which is partially filled by a previous stitch. The loose ends at the beginning and end of the stitching are woven into the previously worked area.

Tent stitch, also called petit point and half cross stitch, is the best known and most popular stitch. It can be used for detailed work, for flat areas of a design, or as a *compensating stitch*, to fill in small areas between other stitches. It is also used over *tramming* to give a hard-wearing ridged appearance. Other basic needlepoint stitches include *cross stitch*, *Gobelin*, *Parisian* and *Hungarian* stitches. The last three are worked vertically with the yarn lying between the upright threads of the canvas, making it essential to use a wool which is thick enough to cover the canvas.

Tent stitch

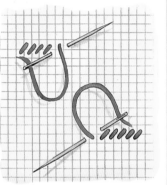

This is the smallest needle-point stitch, worked over one intersection of canvas. Each stitch is made from top right to bottom left. This produces a long thread at the back between stitches which makes the work hard-wearing. For the second row, starting at the right, each stitch is worked from bottom left to top right.

Diagonal tent stitch

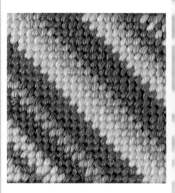

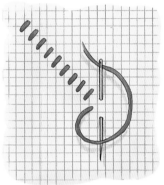

This is worked diagonally from top left downwards to bottom right. The first stitch is made over one intersection, as for tent stitch. Subsequent similar stitches are made diagonally below. For the second row, begin at the bottom, to the left of the first row and work upwards, filling in the spaces.

◀ **Susan Smith**
Oakgates
Tent stitch and Gobelin stitch successfully depict the details on the house and in the sky.

Tramming	Gobelin stitch	Parisian stitch	Hungarian stitch

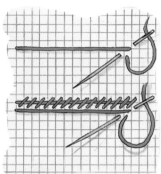	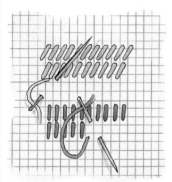	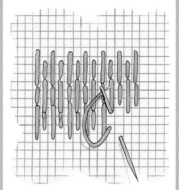	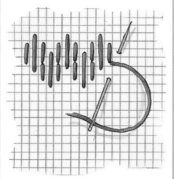

Tramming

This is a long horizontal stitch laid along the double threads of a canvas as a base over which the tent, gobelin or other stitches are worked.

Gobelin stitch

This straight stitch, called after the tapestries of that name, can be worked in a variety of ways, either upright or slightly slanting and stitched over a differing number of horizontal, as well as vertical, threads.

Parisian stitch

This consists of alternating long and short vertical stitches, usually worked over four and two threads respectively. In the second row, the long stitches are worked directly below the short stitches of the previous row, and vice versa.

Hungarian stitch

This forms a half-drop pattern suitable for backgrounds. It consists of groups of three vertical stitches, worked over two, four and again two threads. Two vertical threads are left between each group, into which subsequent rows are interlocked.

Compensating stitches
For pictorial and abstract designs containing irregular or curved shapes, it may not be possible to fill the entire area with a given stitch. Compensating stitches are those which are worked to fill in the gaps around the edges. It is essential to retain the form of the stitch as much as possible, working half or a part of it. Tent stitch is often the best solution for small spaces.

CROSSED STITCHES

Basic cross stitch is well known, but is only one of a number of stitches where threads cross. In each case the top threads should all lie in the same direction, unless there is some aesthetic reason to contradict this rule.

Variations can be made in size and shape – *long-legged, upright cross, herringbone* and *tied Gobelin* are elongated or irregular versions – while others, such as *plaited Gobelin* encroach on the previous row to form the cross.

Areas of crossed stitches produce different textures, from the smoothness of single cross stitch to the raised braid effects of long-legged cross and herringbone stitch. Some, such as upright cross, can combine with other stitches to fill in gaps or can be worked in two colours.

Cross stitch

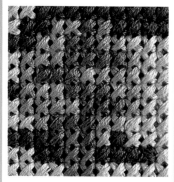

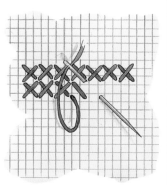

Two diagonal straight stitches are worked over two intersections of canvas at right-angles to one another. Complete each cross before starting the next. If you are working a long row of cross stitch you may prefer to make the first half of the stitches for one row, and then complete them by working back along the row in the reverse direction. Larger versions are unlikely to cover the canvas satisfactorily so may need to be interspersed with other stitches.

Upright cross stitch

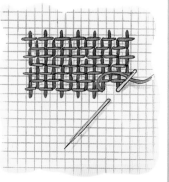

Also known as straight cross stitch, this makes a good texture for backgrounds. It consists of a vertical and a horizontal stitch worked to form a cross over two threads of canvas. The second row of crosses is worked to interlock between those in the first row.

Plaited Gobelin stitch

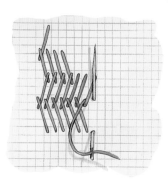

Starting at the bottom left-hand side of the stitch, work a row of slanting Gobelin stitches (page 41) over one vertical and four horizontal threads. The second row slants in the opposite direction, starting three threads below, and crossing the first row. The length and slant of this stitch can be varied.

Tied Gobelin stitch

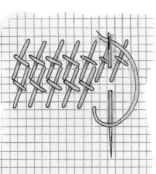

Work a slanting stitch over five horizontal and two vertical threads of canvas. Secure it at its centre with a small stitch made obliquely over one horizontal and two vertical threads. Each long stitch is worked with a space of two threads between it and the next, and the second row of stitches is placed directly below, encroaching by two horizontal threads.

Long-legged cross stitch

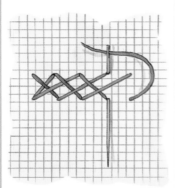

Starting at the bottom left-hand corner of the stitch, take a diagonal stitch over three horizontal and six vertical threads. Bring the needle out immediately below this point and on a level with the starting point. Take a cross stitch diagonally back over three vertical and three horizontal threads. Repeat.

Herringbone stitch

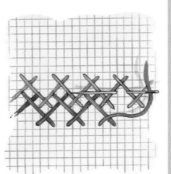

This is similar to surface embroidery herringbone (page 20). Work a diagonal stitch to the right over four intersections of canvas. Then bring the needle out again two vertical threads to the left before making another diagonal stitch, again over four intersections and crossing the first. The second row is worked directly below and encroaches into the first.

▲ **Elizabeth Ashurst**
House on the Hill
Tent, cross, Gobelin and velvet stitch feature in this piece.

DIAGONAL STITCHES

In this group of stitches, each individual stitch is worked diagonally, and the stitches *en masse* form diagonal patterns of varying complexity across the canvas.

Diagonal, cashmere and Moorish stitches are suitable for covering areas of background in an unobtrusive manner, while *Milanese, Jacquard* and *Byzantine* are bolder and can be quite striking, especially if the rows are worked in contrasting threads.

Diagonal stitches are usually shown worked from top left to bottom right, but by reversing the instructions they can be stitched in the other direction.

Diagonal stitch

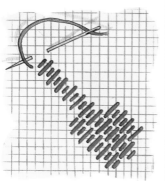

The smaller version of this stitch is made up of diagonal stitches taken over one and two intersections of canvas alternately. The larger version consists of groups of four diagonal stitches worked over two, three, four and three intersections, which are then repeated. Subsequent rows interlock.

Moorish stitch

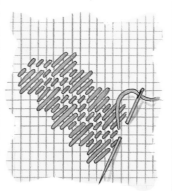

This is an attractive background stitch which can be worked in one or two colours. Rows of large diagonal stitch are interspersed with rows of diagonal tent stitch (page 40).

Cashmere stitch

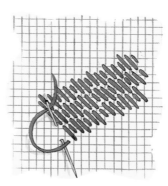

Depending on the effect required, you can vary the oblique line of this stitch. Repeated groups of diagonal stitches are worked alongside one another over one, two, and again two intersections of canvas. Subsequent rows are interlocked with those previously worked.

Milanese stitch

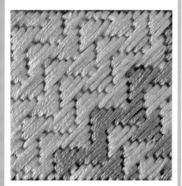

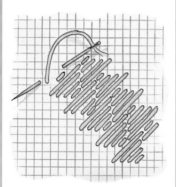

This consists of triangles made up of groups of diagonal stitches worked over one, two, three and four intersections. These are repeated along the diagonal, with subsequent rows reversed and interlocked with the shortest stitch opposite the longest on the previous row.

Byzantine stitch

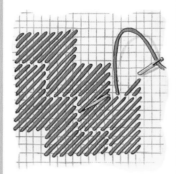

This stitch gives the effect of a series of steps, usually worked from top left. The length, width and direction of the steps may be varied. Five diagonal stitches are made alongside one another over four intersections; then four are worked downwards to form the zigzag. Continue stitching the groups of four stitches, alternating horizontal and vertical.

Jacquard stitch

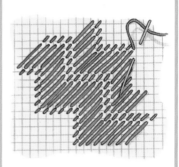

This is a stepped stitch similar to Byzantine, usually with the larger stitches worked over four intersections of canvas. These steps are separated by rows of tent stitch (page 40). As with Byzantine stitch, the height, width and direction of the zigzags can be varied.

▶ **Pauline Brown**
A sampler showing Byzantine and Jacquard stitches worked in different directions.

EYELETS

Eyelets are normally worked in a square over an even number of threads in each directon. The stitches are taken from the outer edge of the square down into the central hole. To keep the centre well defined, it is sometimes necessary to enlarge it slightly with a stiletto before beginning. The thread chosen for eyelets should be fairly fine and tightly spun, so that it will not form too much bulk in the centre hole.

Square and *rectangular eyelets* can both be worked in the normal way or varied by moving the hole off-centre and working over any number of threads.

Diamond eyelets form a half-drop pattern when stitched in rows. They can be outlined with straight stitches to emphasize the diamond effect.

Fan stitch is worked in a similar way to eyelets, except that the stitches fan out from the corner hole. It can be worked in any direction, producing a variety of different patterns.

Circular eyelets can be used as individual motifs, such as flowers, or as an all-over pattern, either in one colour or in a range of hues.

Square eyelets

Starting at the top right-hand corner, work radiating stitches in an anti-clockwise direction around a square consisting of an even number of threads. Take the needle down into the centre hole for each stitch, and bring it up at the edge of the square.

Diamond eyelets

These are worked in a similar way to conventional square eyelets. The vertical and horizontal stitches are made over five threads of canvas, with the other stitches between worked diagonally into the centre hole. Diamond eyelets can be used individually to represent flowers or can be used as an all-over pattern, sometimes outlined with long diagonal stitches.

Fan stitch

Fan stitch is usually worked over three vertical and three horizontal threads of canvas. It is actually a quarter of a square eyelet, with stitches radiating from a corner hole. The direction and size of the stitch can be varied.

Circular eyelets

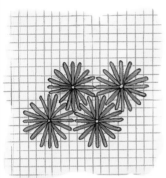

These are stitched in a similar way to conventional square eyelets. However, they form an octagonal shape, consisting of 16 radiating stitches. The whole stitch is worked over six horizontal and six vertical threads of canvas – each side of the octagon has three radiating stitches.

Variation on circular eyelets

Circular eyelets can be worked side by side with subsequent rows interlocking to produce an all-over pattern. If the second row is worked immediately below the first, the resultant spaces can be filled with smaller eyelets.

Eyelet variations

Eyelets are so versatile that it is worth experimenting with different sizes and shapes, and the effect of moving the hole off-centre.

▲ **Eyelet ribbon embroidery**
Pauline Brown
Narrow satin and metallic ribbons are worked on canvas using conventional needlepoint stitches with French knots added.

SQUARE STITCHES

A number of needlepoint stitches have a square shape as their main characteristic, which makes them suitable, among other things, for creating architectural features such as stone or brickwork.

Cushion stitch is especially versatile, as it can be worked in either direction and any size. Large-scale versions can be further varied with an additional stitch or series of stitches worked across in the other direction to form *crossed cushion stitch*.

When cushion stitch is outlined with tent stitch it becomes *Scottish stitch*, which is useful for depicting windows or tiles.

Rice stitch, also known as crossed corners, is worked in two stages over an even number of threads. A contrasting colour can be used for the corner stitches.

Smyrna or double cross stitch is also stitched over an even number of threads. It should be kept to a small size so as to cover the canvas adequately.

Cushion stitch

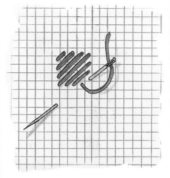

Groups of diagonal stitches are worked over first one, two, three and four, then three, two and one intersections to form a square. Variations can be made in size or direction.

Crossed cushion stitch

There are two versions of this stitch, in each case worked on top of individual cushion stitches or groups of the required size. The first variation consists of a single diagonal stitch worked in the reverse direction from corner to corner over cushion stitch. For a padded effect, one half of the cushion stitch can be covered with diagonal stitches worked in the reverse direction.

Scottish stitch

Rows of cushion stitch are separated with a grid of tent stitch. The size of the cushion stitch and the colours used can be varied to produce a more random effect.

Rice stitch

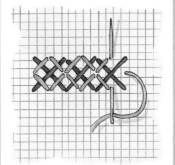

Work a large cross stitch (page 42) over four intersections of canvas. Then work small diagonal stitches over two intersections across each corner. Slight variations in size and colour can be made.

Smyrna stitch

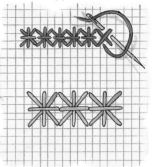

This consists of a cross stitch (page 42) worked over two or four intersections of canvas, with an upright cross stitch (page 42) stitched on top. If working conventionally, the top stitches should all lie in one direction, either horizontal or vertical.

◄ **Anna Christy**
Rhodes Fragment II
Cushion and fan stitch are included in this piece, which has been machine embroidered on to a linen background.

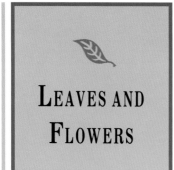

LEAVES AND FLOWERS

Many embroiderers enjoy creating needlepoint pictures of gardens and floral subjects. In addition to circular and diamond eyelets (page 46), a number of stitches lend themselves to these effects.

Leaf stitch is versatile and suitable for individual leaves and small-scale trees; it can be worked as an all-over pattern with the leaf shapes interlocking, or four can be stitched to form a star.

Petal stitch is a square-shaped stitch which can also be worked diagonally in diamond form. The circular weaving stitches raise the "petals" to give a flower-like effect.

Pinwheel stitch is an attractive variation of Milanese stitch (page 45), useful for large-scale flower heads. It can be used alone or in conjunction with other stitches.

Fantail stitch is similar to half a large circular eyelet, with additional stitches forming the "stem". It makes a useful all-over pattern of flower shapes.

Leaf stitch

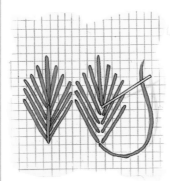

To work in an upright position, begin with a vertical stitch over six horizontal threads. On either side of this, make three diagonal stitches, starting one thread down and one to the side, and inserting the needle below the vertical stitch. Working downwards, make two more diagonal stitches of equal length on each side over three vertical and five horizontal threads.

▶ **Pauline Brown**
Detail of *Herbaceous Border* (see page 131) with leaf stitch worked in various sizes and yarns, as well as ribbon.

Leaf stitch variations

For an all-over pattern, the first rows of leaf stitches are worked side by side with subsequent rows interlocked. Sizes and shapes can be varied, and spaces can be filled with compensating tent stitches.

Leaf stitch star

This consists of four leaf stitches worked towards a central point. A long stitch can be added along the centre of each leaf if required.

Diagonal leaf stitch

This is worked in a similar way to upright leaf stitch, starting with a diagonal stitch worked over four intersections. An all-over pattern can be built up, and a star-shaped version made with four leaves.

Petal stitch

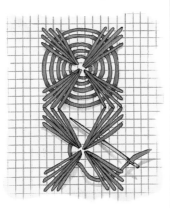

When worked over ten threads of canvas, this square stitch has five stitches radiating from the centre at each corner, in a similar way to the corners of eyelet stitch (page 46). The second part of the stitch, which can be worked in contrasting thread, involves winding the thread around the centre hole several times, passing under the diagonal stitches.

Pinwheel stitch

This is worked in a similar way to Milanese stitch (page 45) but with four triangles meeting at a central point. Each of these is made with four diagonal stitches worked over one, two, three and four intersections. Between these, four more triangles of four horizontal or vertical stitches are worked.

Fantail stitch

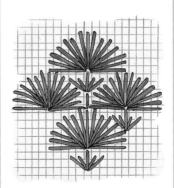

The semi-circular "eyelet" is worked over ten vertical and five horizontal threads with fifteen stitches radiating from the centre hole. The stem is made with straight and diagonal stitches which fill in the gaps when the stitch is worked as an all-over pattern.

TEXTURED STITCHES

An innovation in recent years has been the introduction of texture to complement the inherent smooth effect of needlepoint. This can be achieved in two ways.

Surface embroidery stitches can be worked, either following the mesh of the canvas or disregarding it by working over a previously stitched area. Some of the most popular stitches for this type of effect are bullion and French knots, chain and whipped chain (pages 30 and 17), but any other surface stitch can be used.

There are also a few needlepoint stitches which create texture, one being *velvet stitch*. This produces loops which can be cut to give a tufted pile, and is useful for a wide range of subjects from fluffy animals to the centres of flowers.

Rhodes stitch, named after its creator, Mary Rhodes, is a versatile bulky stitch worked over any number of threads. Large-scale versions can be secured in a similar way to crossed cushion (page 48), with diagonal stitches worked across the corners.

You can also embroider just half a Rhodes stitch, in which case you will need other stitches such as tent (page 40) or straight stitches to fill in the gaps. For *half Rhodes half-drop*, subsequent rows interlock to form an overall pattern.

Norwich stitch, also known as waffle stitch, consists of a series of diagonal stitches worked in rotation to form an interwoven square. Both Rhodes and Norwich stitch lend themselves to bold geometric designs.

Norwich stitch

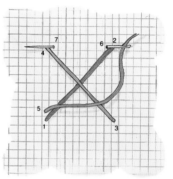

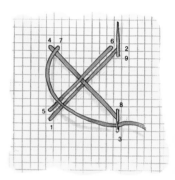

1 This is worked over a square with an uneven number of threads of canvas. Start with a cross stitch from corner to corner, then bring the needle out one thread up from the beginning, making a diagonal stitch alongside the first stitch.

2 Bring the needle out one thread to the right of the second stitch and make the next stitch alongside the second.

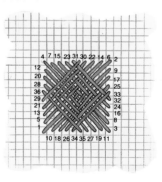

3 Continue working a series of parallel stitches round the square.

Rhodes stitch

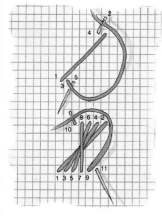

1 Begin with a diagonal stitch across the square; bring out the needle one thread to the right of where you began and insert it one thread to the left of, and crossing, the first diagonal stitch.

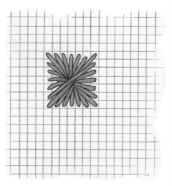

2 Continue working anti-clockwise round the square, crossing the previously worked stitches until the area is completed.

Rhodes stitch variations

The corners of Rhodes stitch can be held down with diagonal stitches of the same or contrasting yarn. Half Rhodes stitches can be interspersed with tent stitch or upright Gobelin. Half Rhodes half-drop consists of rows of half normal Rhodes stitches worked side by side, with the second row encroaching halfway down the first.

Velvet stitch

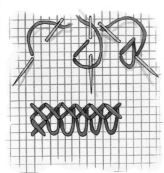

Work a half cross stitch from bottom left to top right over one or two intersections. Repeat this stitch, leaving a loose loop, and hold it down with the thumb of the non-working hand. Then complete the other half of the holding cross stitch going from bottom right to top left. The loop can either be left or cut to give the velvet-pile effect. Complete the bottom row first, and work towards the top of the area to be filled.

BARGELLO EMBROIDERY

Several theories exist as to the origins of Bargello work, also known as Florentine embroidery, flame stitch and Hungarian point – one legend being that it was brought to Italy when a Medici nobleman married a Hungarian bride in the 15th century.

The distinctive repeating patterns of this type of needlepoint are all worked on single canvas with vertical stitches, usually in wool. Other types of yarn can be used, but bear in mind that straight stitches do not cover the canvas as thoroughly as diagonal ones.

This technique relies for much of its effect on the shading of the colours. The patterns fall into two main categories, those worked across the canvas in curved or zigzag rows, and motif or medallion designs. In both cases, all the stitches are the same length, except when embroidering Hungarian point designs which consist of rows of long stitches interspersed with short ones.

Bargello embroidery is suitable for both decorative panels and a number of practical items such as cushions and chair seats, shopping and evening bags. In such cases the stitches should be restricted to a fairly short length to avoid snagging.

Charting a design
Unless you are working experimentally with no formal pattern, line charts are used for Bargello embroidery – it is only necessary to work out one row of the basic repeat pattern, which can then be worked as many times as necessary across the canvas. Subsequent horizontal rows usually follow the contours of this foundation row exactly.

In the case of symmetrical motifs, only the top half needs to be charted, as the lower half is a mirror image – it is in fact a help to use a mirror to establish the appearance of a motif.

Since Bargello embroidery is usually symmetrical, it is practical to begin in the centre of a row, stitch to the right and then return to the centre prior to working the left-hand side. This allows you to refer across to the previously worked area in order to keep the stitches in line.

Bargello stitch

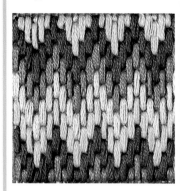

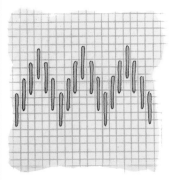

Generally worked vertically, over an even number of threads, Bargello stitch resembles upright Gobelin (page 41). The most usual size is over four horizontal threads, with the next stitch dropping down two threads, but this can be varied to produce differing patterns.

▶ **Fiona Lewis**
A random approach to working Bargello embroidery.

Zigzags and curves

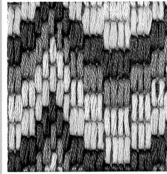

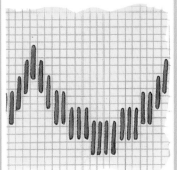

The simplest Bargello zigzag design is produced with stitches of similar size, dropping down or extending upwards across the canvas in a regular manner. For a shallower zigzag, two or more stitches are worked at each level. Curves are made with two or three stitches worked in steps on the same level towards and at the top or bottom of a zigzag.

Motif (or medallion) designs

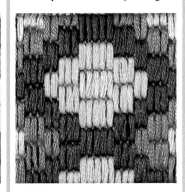

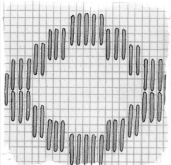

To establish a motif, place two mirrors at right-angles to each other on a charted design, and slide them along until a suitable motif appears. Draw in the horizontal and vertical perimeters of the shape and re-draw, incorporating the mirrored design.

Hungarian point pattern

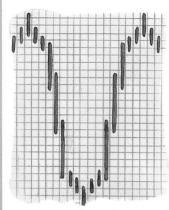

This is a spiky zigzag pattern made up of groups of both long and short vertical stitches alternating in the same row. The long stitches are usually over four or six threads, while the short are worked over two.

Pinnacle pattern

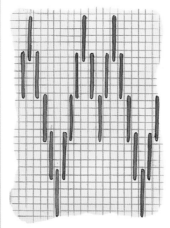

The pointed effects of pinnacle patterns are created with long stitches, usually over six threads. Each one drops down or extends upwards over five threads in steep steps.

▲ **Fiona Lewis**
Needlepoint sampler with a surround of Hungarian point pattern.

FOUR-WAY BARGELLO

In this attractive variation of Bargello embroidery the pattern is stitched in each direction to form a radiating design of four identical triangles. Rows of curves and zigzags, or motifs can both be adapted to form this four-way modification.

As with normal Bargello work, the main structure of the design can be charted on graph paper, and if two mirrors are used to help formulate the design, only a quarter of it need be drawn. It is best to establish the design some way from the centre point. Subsequent rows of stitching can follow the shape exactly as you work towards the centre and then outwards to cover the surrounding area.

Compensating stitches (page 41) will be needed to complete the diagonal and the outer edges.

▶ **Joyce Robertson**
Four-way Bargello makes an attractive little cushion.

Preparing the canvas

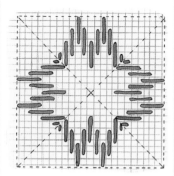

Mark the canvas by drawing or tacking two diagonal lines from corner to corner plus perpendicular lines across the centre.

Stitching the design

To establish the pattern in the top quarter, start some way above the mid-point and in the centre of a row, stitching towards the right-hand diagonal line. Return to the centre and complete the row to the left. Repeat this pattern in the other three directions. It may be necessary to make small compensating stitches where the quarters join. Work towards the centre and then complete the surrounding area by repeating the first row and changing the colour as necessary.

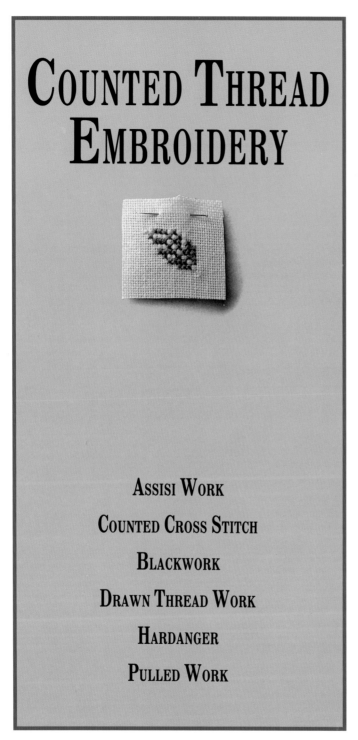

COUNTED THREAD EMBROIDERY

ASSISI WORK

COUNTED CROSS STITCH

BLACKWORK

DRAWN THREAD WORK

HARDANGER

PULLED WORK

Counted thread embroidery is a generic term for a number of techniques. In each technique, a stitch is worked over an exact number of threads, resulting in designs which tend to be precise and often geometric. Included in this category are counted cross stitch, Assisi work, pulled and drawn thread work, Hardanger and blackwork.

Fabrics
All counted thread methods are stitched on evenweave fabric, which is woven with the same number of horizontal (weft) threads as the vertical (warp) threads. Specialist embroidery evenweaves are usually cotton or linen with a range of from 12 to 32 threads per 2.5 cm (1 in). Some fabrics such as Aida and Hardanger fabric are made with groups of threads woven together.

Needles
Tapestry needles (available in sizes 13–24) should always be used for counted thread methods. They have blunt points and large eyes and slip easily between the weave of the fabric without splitting the fibres.

Frames
Counted thread work should always be mounted in a frame. If a circular embroidery hoop is used, care must be taken to ensure that the warp and weft are not distorted.

Box charts
These are used for designing cross stitch and Assisi work as well as for tent stitch needlepoint patterns. Each square on graph paper represents one stitch, with either symbols or colours defining different coloured areas in the design.

ASSISI WORK

Originating in the Italian town of that name, the particular characteristic of Assisi work is that the motifs are enclosed with double running stitch, sometimes called Holbein stitch, or back stitch, usually in a dark thread. The entire background area is then covered with cross stitch in a contrasting mid tone. Additional details are sometimes added in double running stitch. Designs should be worked out on graph paper.

Fabric
Use evenly woven cotton, linen or wool, including embroidery evenweaves of either single or double thread construction. Unless the piece of embroidery is very small, it should be framed for working.

Threads
Coton à broder, stranded cotton or pearl cotton, which is a similar thickness to or thinner than the weave of the background fabric, should be used.

Needles
Tapestry needles should be used.

Following a box chart

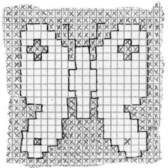

Box charts are drawn on to squared paper with each square representing a single stitch, such as a cross or a tent stitch. The squares are either filled in with the intended colours, or symbols representing the colours are used. This type of chart is normally used for counted cross stitch, Assisi work and needlepoint designs worked entirely in tent stitch.

Double running stitch

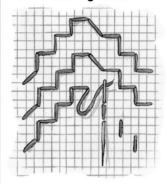

Working from the box chart, it is usual to begin by stitching the outlines of the design in double running stitch. Make the outline of single running stitches each over two threads of fabric. Then work another row of running stitches into the same holes, but filling in the gaps left in the first line.

Cross stitch

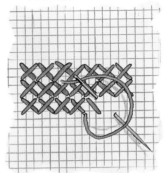

Once the outlines are completed, cross stitch is used to cover the background areas, leaving the motif as a "negative" area. The cross stitch is worked as in needlepoint (page 38), over two threads of fabric, keeping the top thread on each stitch slanting in the same direction.

▼ **Pauline Brown**
A reversed repeat motif taken from peasant-style embroidery.

COUNTED CROSS STITCH

This is one of the most familiar of embroidery techniques, relying for its effect on clearly defined designs and good choice of colour. It is used in peasant embroidery in many parts of the world, and in England counted cross stitch became popular for samplers in the 18th and 19th centuries.

Fabrics
Evenweave fabric in cotton or linen, with from 12 to 34 threads per 2.5 cm (1 in) is ideal. Usually cross stitch is worked over two threads, with the fabric's degree of fineness determining the size of the stitch. With fabrics such as Aida and Hardanger, which are woven with groups of threads forming the weave, it is usual to stitch over one intersection only. Small pieces of cross stitch can be worked in the hand, but it is advisable to frame up larger-scale work.

Threads and needles
Choose a thread similar to or finer than the coarseness of the fabric. Stranded cotton, silk and coton à broder produce clearly defined stitches. For larger-scale work, fine tapestry wools, linen or crochet yarns can be used. Tapestry needles of suitable size should be used.

Designs
Counted cross stitch is a favourite method for producing alphabets, and decorative borders featuring either flowers or abstract patterns. There are a large number of cross stitch kits on the market, but it is more rewarding to produce individual designs using original drawings, photographs or photocopies. Designs can be worked out using a box chart made by tracing the subject onto transparent graph paper.

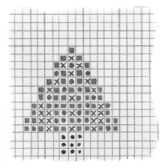

Work out your design on graph paper, make any final adjustments and then use this as a guide for your embroidery.

Though it is usual to work over two threads of fabric when stitching on evenweave linen, cross stitch can in fact be done over any number of threads.

On Aida or similar fabrics which have groups of threads woven in a type of basket weave, stitches are normally worked over a single intersection.

Starting and finishing cross stitch
This method can be used for all types of counted thread embroidery. Begin by leaving a short length of thread on the right side. After a few stitches, pull this to the back of the work, thread it in a needle and darn it into the back of three or four stitches. Finishing off is done in the same way, with the thread darned through the back of the previously worked stitches.

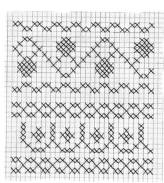

▲ Border

An example of a border design

► Susan Smith

Mauve Valentine

Counted cross stitch is a useful medium for lettering and for detailed designs. Here it is combined with pulled work.

▼ ABC

An example of a cross stitch alphabet.

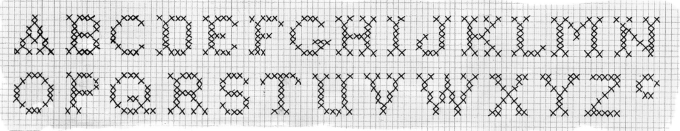

BLACKWORK

Blackwork, sometimes known as Spanish blackwork, is said to have been introduced to Britain by Henry VIII's Spanish wife Catherine of Aragon. Certainly it appears extensively on Tudor costume.

It is a counted thread method based on vertical, horizontal and diagonal back stitches or running stitches, which form decorative geometric patterns.

Fabrics
Specialist embroidery evenweaves in cotton or linen with 22 to 26 threads per 2.5 cm (1 in) are the most suitable for traditional style work, but any smooth-surfaced evenly woven fabric can be used for a freer approach. Framing the work will help to achieve good tension.

Threads and needles
This technique is usually worked in black thread – hence the name – sometimes with the addition of red or gold details. In contemporary work a limited palette of other colours is sometimes introduced.

Use tapestry needles, and smooth-textured threads such as coton à broder, stranded cotton or pearl cotton which are similar to or finer than the weave of the background fabric. Fine lurex metallic threads or filament yarns are suitable for details.

Designs
Traditionally designs have been based on geometric patterns filling the main areas which are outlined in back stitch – or for heavier lines in chain or stem stitches (page 16). These can be worked out on graph paper using a box chart (page 59). Freestyle designs which include a limited number of outlines and changes in density of stitch can be marked on the fabric with an erasable marker.

Back stitch

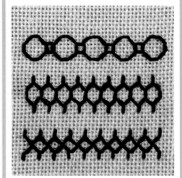

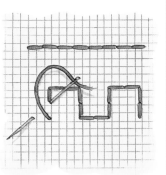

This is worked as for surface embroidery (page 14), but usually over two threads of fabric. For blackwork, the stitch can be worked horizontally, vertically or diagonally, and as there is no recognized sequence of stitching, it is necessary to devise the most logical way of embroidering each individual pattern.

Algerian eye stitch

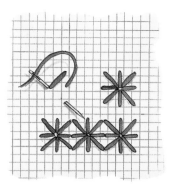

Starting at the top right-hand corner, work radiating stitches in a clockwise direction around a square consisting of four threads. The needle is taken down into the centre hole for each stitch and brought up at the edge of the square.

Creating tone

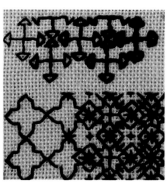

Gradations of tone can be achieved in two main ways, the first being to use threads of varying thicknesses for the same stitch. The second method, when using an all-over geometric design, involves progressively omitting more and more of the pattern.

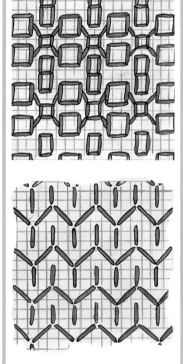

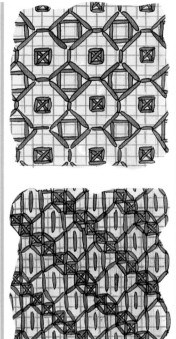

◄ **Blackwork**
Different types of blackwork pattern.

◄ **Amanda Ewing**
Two Dogs
The diminishing density of the pattern creates the form and shading of the animals.

DRAWN THREAD WORK

This type of embroidery is most often used for items of table linen. As its name indicates, the technique involves withdrawing threads from the background fabric to produce a delicate openwork effect. Either the warp or the weft threads are removed and decorative stitches are then worked over the remaining threads, forming borders or bands.

The foundation of most drawn thread work is hem stitching. This is worked on either side of the band of withdrawn threads and holds groups of the remaining fabric threads together. Open corners are made by with-drawing bands of both warp and weft threads. These can be treated decoratively with needlewoven effects.

Fabrics
For table linen choose evenweave linen or cotton which is sufficiently loosely woven for the threads to be withdrawn easily. Other fabrics such as furnishing sheers (a loosely-woven fabric) or hessian could be used for less practical items such as wallhangings. Correct tension is best achieved if the work is framed.

Threads and needles
For traditional hem stitching use cotton or linen thread, choosing the colour and texture that closely matches the background fabric. For a freer approach any thread can be used. Work with tapestry needles of a suitable size.

Designs
Because of the nature of the technique, designs are mainly restricted to borders, squares or rectangles. Bands of stitchery can also be worked either parallel or at right-angles to each other. For a precise design which needs to be centred, mark the centre with a line of tacking; then tack along both edges of the areas to be withdrawn.

Preparation

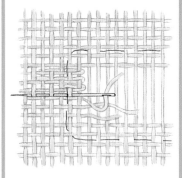

Mark the centre and tack precisely around the area where the threads are to be removed. With a small pair of embroidery scissors, carefully cut the horizontal threads at the centre. Withdraw these using a tapestry needle and leaving the exact number of vertical threads required. Darn the withdrawn threads a short distance into the fabric at either end and trim off the excess.

Hem stitching

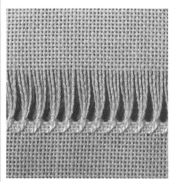

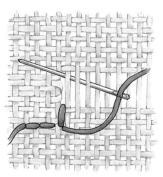

1 Darn the working thread between several vertical threads and bring the needle out two or three threads below the left-hand end of the open area.

2 Pick up three or four vertical threads and, encircling these, insert the needle to the right from the back, bringing it out again two threads below.

Ladder stitch	Zigzag hem stitch	Double hem stitch	Interlaced hem stitch
		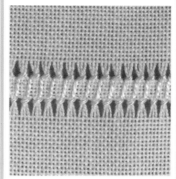	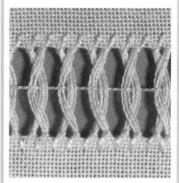
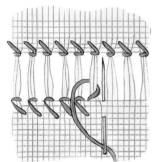	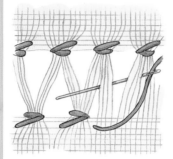	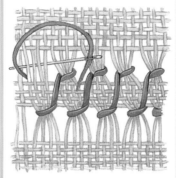	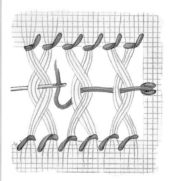
This consists of ordinary hem stitching worked either side of a withdrawn band, so that the same group of threads is bound on each side.	Work hem stitch along the lower edge of a withdrawn band, making sure that each group contains an even number of vertical threads. Then turn the work and hem stitch the other edge, grouping the threads so that half are taken from each adjacent group.	This is worked between two bands of withdrawn threads, with four to six threads of fabric left between them. Starting from the right, back stitch over three or four threads at the top of the lower withdrawn band. Then make a diagonal stitch on the back of the work, bring the needle out at the bottom of the top band and make a back stitch over the same three or four threads. Repeat.	Hem stitch both edges of a wide withdrawn band as for ladder stitch. For the interlacing, fasten the thread in the centre of the right-hand end. Take the needle from left to right under the second group of threads, then over the first group. Bring the needle forward, twisting the groups of threads. Repeat.

Preparation

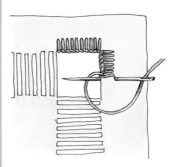

The open space which results when threads are withdrawn in both directions can be decorated in a variety of ways. Cut and withdraw two sets of threads, one group horizontally and the other vertically. Darn in the ends (page 64) and reinforce the two outer edges of the space with buttonhole stitch (page 20). Work the chosen hem stitching along both lengths of the withdrawn threads.

Spider's web corner

1 Make a cross stitch (page 42) across the open corner, fastening off firmly; overcast one diagonal stitch, and then overcast half-way along the other.

2 Work a spider's web (page 28) on this base of four stitches. Finish by completing the overcasting on the second diagonal stitch.

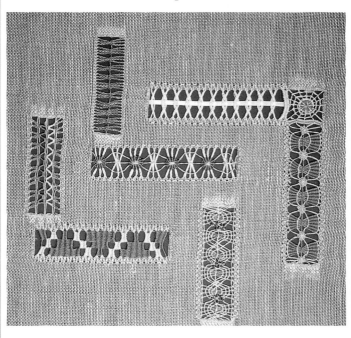

▲ Sarah Cookson
This sampler displays stitches of varying complexity and uses coloured threads.

Woven corner

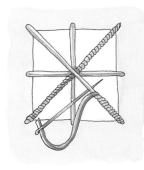

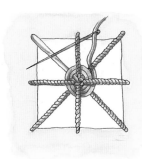

1 This is particularly suitable for incorporating with interlaced hem stitching. Extend the threads used for the interlacing right to the edge of the open area and then make a cross stitch to form a double cross stitch at the corner. Overcast one diagonal stitch, and then overcast half-way along the other.

2 Then start weaving as for woven wheels (page 28). Finish by completing the overcasting on the second diagonal stitch.

Needleweaving

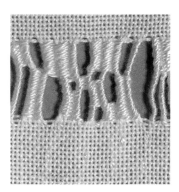

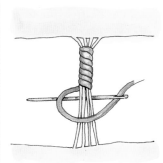

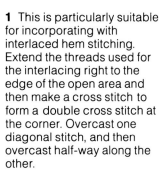

1 Groups of threads can be overcast or woven together either informally or in precise patterns. Overcasting consists of wrapping a group of threads in a withdrawn area with the working thread.

2 When weaving, groups of threads are darned back and forth. These can be pulled away from the perpendicular for an irregular effect, or patterns simulating woven motifs can be created.

HARDANGER

This type of openwork counted thread embroidery takes its name from a mountainous district in Norway. It is characterized by rectangular groups of satin stitches known as "kloster blocks", which enclose the cut areas.

Remaining bars of warp or weft threads are usually needlewoven together, and open centres may be embroidered in a similar way to drawn thread work corners (pages 66–7). Additional satin stitch patterns such as stars are sometimes worked on the areas surrounding the kloster blocks.

Hardanger is most often used for table linen embroidered in white or cream threads or threads which tone with the background fabric.

Fabrics
A specialist embroidery evenweave known as Hardanger fabric is used. This, which is firmly woven with double threads, is available in a variety of colours.

Threads and needles
Choose a matching or toning thread such as pearl cotton, which is of a similar weight to the Hardanger fabric. Use a tapestry needle of suitable size for the thread.

Designs
Hardanger designs are invariably geometric as it is difficult to work this technique freely. Kloster blocks can take the form of squares, diamonds and triangles which are drawn on a line chart (page 39). Shade in the areas which are to be cut away.

▲ **Margaret Rivers**
An example of Hardanger showing kloster blocks with overcast and woven bars, together with loop stitch filling. Also included are spider's web corners (page 67).

Kloster blocks

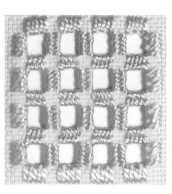

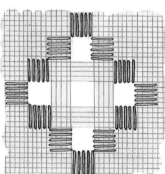

Groups of horizontal and vertical satin stitches are worked to enclose areas which are subsequently cut away. The simplest form is a square consisting of groups of five stitches worked over four threads and placed at right-angles to one another. A diamond block can be made with 12 similar groups of satin stitch.

Cutting and withdrawing threads

When the kloster blocks have been completed, parts of the area which they enclose are carefully withdrawn and cut away. This is done in a similar way to drawn thread work (page 64), but the ends are trimmed and not darned in. Only those threads which are at right-angles to the ends of the satin stitches are cut away.

Woven and overcast bars

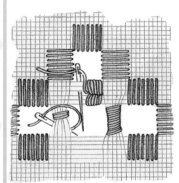

When groups of threads are withdrawn in a kloster block, a number of loose ones are left between areas of fabric. These are either needlewoven or overcast as for drawn thread work (page 64).

Loop stitch

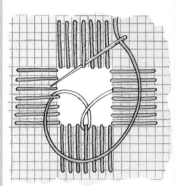

Worked in the open square left by the withdrawn threads, a loosely tensioned buttonhole stitch is made through the middle stitch of each group of satin stitches. Loop stitch can also be worked over overcast bars.

Additional decoration

Satin stitch surface decoration can be worked around or adjoining the cut areas. Blocks, diamonds, stars, pyramids and mitres incorporate horizontal, vertical or diagonal stitches.

PULLED WORK

Also known as pulled thread work and drawn fabric, this type of embroidery probably began as an imitation of lace, with texture and pattern being the most important features.

The technique differs from drawn thread embroidery (page 64) in that the openwork effect is achieved, not by withdrawing threads, but by pulling some threads together and others apart.

Pulled work is suitable for table linen, and can also be useful for combining with other techniques, such as surface stitchery, to add texture to otherwise undecorated backgrounds.

Fabrics
Although it is traditionally embroidered on evenweave linen with stitches carefully counted, it can also be worked in a more random fashion on loosely woven fabrics such as scrim or furnishing sheers. Tension is an important aspect of pulled work, and the fabric should thus be framed before commencing.

Threads and needles
For conventional pulled work choose a strong thread which matches the background fabric – threads can be withdrawn from the background and used for the stitching. Coton à broder, button thread, crochet cotton and pearl cotton are all suitable, used in a tapestry needle of suitable size.

Designs
While traditional designs are generally based on geometric forms, a more contemporary approach features random blocks of pulled work patterns. Either way the design can be marked on the fabric with tacking stitches or with an erasable marker.

▼ **Lydia Solomon**
A variety of pulled work stitches on a loosely woven fabric.

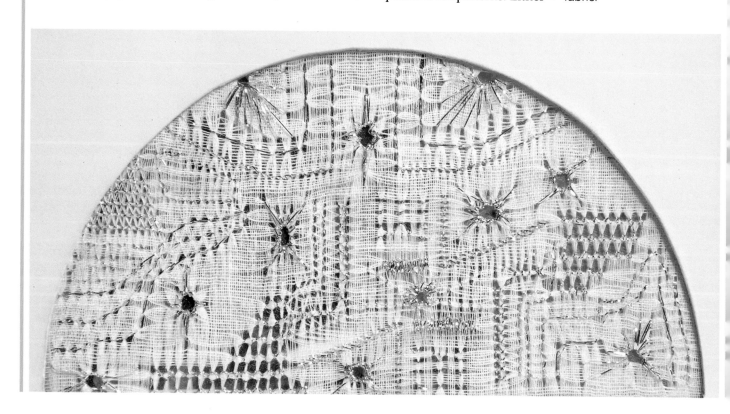

Tension	Chessboard filling	Small chessboard filling	Step stitch
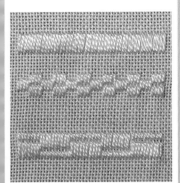	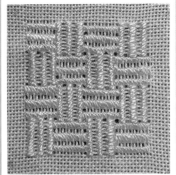		
	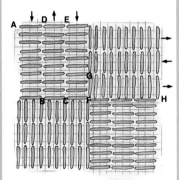	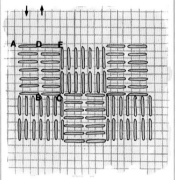	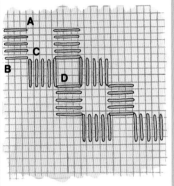

An important aspect of pulled work is the tension of the individual stitches. In most cases the thread is pulled tightly, bringing the fabric threads together and creating patterns of holes.

For clarity, however, line charts usually depict the stitches with a slack tension as for other counted thread methods. The effects of different tensions are most easily seen when working satin stitch. If the thread is left untensioned (top), it appears as a wide band on the surface. If it is pulled tight (bottom), a row of holes appears either side of the narrow band. Satin stitch is the basis for a range of fillings.

Chessboard filling

This consists of blocks of alternating vertical and horizontal satin stitches. Each block comprises three rows of ten satin stitches worked over three fabric threads. Work the rows consecutively in the direction shown.

Small chessboard filling

A smaller version of chessboard filling can be worked in double rows consisting of seven stitches made over three threads. The thread in both chessboard fillings may be pulled tight or remain slack.

Step stitch

This is worked diagonally with blocks of five satin stitches made over four threads alternating in direction in a step formation. Start the first horizontal block at A, finishing at B, then the first vertical block at C ending at D, and so on.

Single faggot stitch

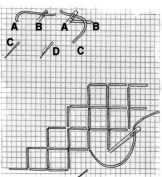

This consists of a series of tensioned back stitches worked diagonally in steps, usually over four threads. Bring the needle out at top right at A, insert it four threads to the right at B. Then bring it out at C (four threads below A) and insert it again at A, before bringing it out four threads to the left of C at D. Repeat. For the second row, turn the work and repeat the stitch alongside the first row, using the adjacent holes made by the first row.

Wave stitch

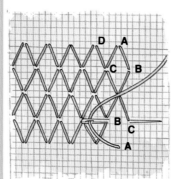

A series of tensioned diagonal back stitches are worked in horizontal lines over an even number of threads. Working from the right, bring the needle out at A, insert it at B diagonally four threads down and two to the right; then bring it out at C (four threads to the left). Insert it again at A and bring it out at D (four threads to the left).

Window filling

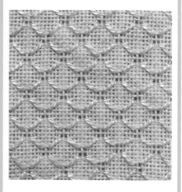

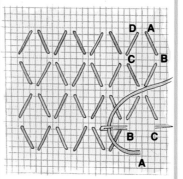

A variation on wave stitch, worked over an uneven number of threads, with one thread left between the stitches. Bring the needle up at A, insert it at B (four threads down and two to the right), bring it out at C (five threads to the left) and insert it at D (one thread to the left of A). One thread is left between each row.

Eyelets

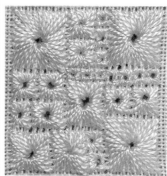

These are stitched in a similar way to those worked on canvas (page 46), with a series of stitches converging in the centre hole, which can be enlarged with a stiletto. The thread can be pulled tight or left untensioned.

Diamond eyelets

This variation worked as for needlepoint (page 46) can be used as a filling stitch or stitched as individual diamond shapes. The thread may be pulled tight or left slack.

Single cross eyelets

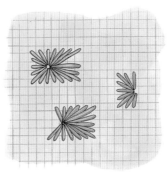

These are worked in a similar way to conventional eyelets, but a single thread is left between each quarter of the eyelet.

Freestyle eyelets

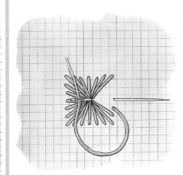

Variations on eyelets can be made by altering the shape, and moving the hole off-centre. For some the thread can be pulled tight, while for others it is left slack.

▶ **Kathryn Francis**
Coloured threads create a different effect from that of the more traditional self-coloured method in this pulled work.

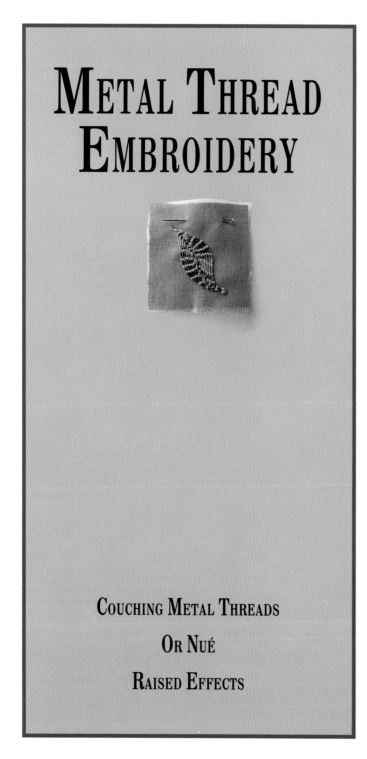

METAL THREAD EMBROIDERY

COUCHING METAL THREADS

OR NUÉ

RAISED EFFECTS

The great age of metal thread ecclesiastical embroidery, the "Opus Anglicanum" of the Middle Ages, is renowned throughout the world. Since then, gold and silver threads have been used whenever a sense of richness is required, whether for religious, court or everyday purposes.

Metal thread (or goldwork) embroidery is regarded by many people as beyond their capabilities. However, it is really just a question of learning to manipulate the metal threads and working neatly to a small scale. The majority of the threads are laid on the background fabric and couched in place. Gold wires and plate can also be incorporated, as can beads and jewels.

Fabrics
Because of the weight of the threads, a closely woven fabric supported on a firm backing is required. Appliqué fabrics in silk, or small pieces of gold and silver kid are often added, with felt and coloured string used for padding. It is essential to frame up the background fabric so that the surface is drum-tight.

Threads
Gold, silver and copper threads come in a wide variety of qualities and types. Many are now processed in synthetic materials, which have the advantage of not tarnishing, but they lack rigidity and the aesthetic qualities of those which contain real metal.

Jap gold, originally made with a paper-thin strip of beaten gold wound round a silk core, has a beautiful lustre, while crinkle, twist and various cords and braids can add texture to a design. Purls, which are tiny coils of metal cut into short lengths, are used as flexible beads.

For stitching the metal threads in place, use a matching sewing silk or cotton.

Needles
Use fine crewel needles for couching, plus a large-eyed chenille needle for taking the metal threads through to the wrong side. Beading needles are required for attaching purls.

Designs
As with other types of surface embroidery, designs should be well planned. Couching of metal threads, although linear, can fill whole areas with richness and cause a play of light on the surface. Texture can be achieved with the use of beads, purls and padded areas. The design should be marked on the background fabric using a fabric marker.

COUCHING METAL THREADS

The principal technique used in metal thread embroidery is couching (page 77). Because of the rigidity of the threads, however, the methods used are not quite the same as those used for couching wool or silk. When applying *fine thread* or *cord*, two strands are usually couched simultaneously, giving a smooth line and covering the surface more quickly. *Braids* and *thicker cords* are stitched singly. While stitching, it is necessary to hold the metal thread taut. The ends are left on the surface until that area of the design has been completed, and are then taken through to the wrong side. *Pearl purl*, which is a rigid metal coil, and *plate*, a flat strip of metal, are treated differently in that they cannot be taken through to the wrong side of the background fabric.

Basic method

Position two strands of fine metal thread at the start of the stitching line, leaving the ends on the surface. Using a fine silk or cotton thread in matching colour, couch over both threads at 6 mm (¼ in) intervals. To finish off the ends, thread each one separately into a chenille needle and pull it through to the back of the work. Oversew the ends on the wrong side.

Corners

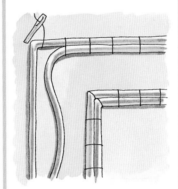

To manipulate a stiff metal thread around a corner, insert the needle on the inner side of the outer thread and pull the thread around it so that it bends at a right-angle. Couch the outer thread with a diagonal stitch. Repeat the bending and diagonal couching process with the inner thread. Continue the couching as normal.

Points

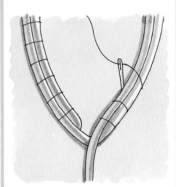

To turn an acute point or corner, bend and couch the outer thread as for turning corners, with a diagonal stitch at the point. Cut the inner thread, take it through to the back of the work at the corner and secure it, then bring it back to the surface and restart it to dovetail alongside the outer thread. Continue couching both threads together.

Couching in a circle

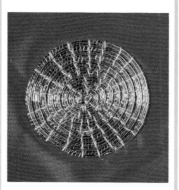

In order to retain the shape and a smooth outline, stagger the starting point of the double threads at the outer edge. Gradually work towards the centre of the circle, couching at regular intervals so that the couching stitches converge in a pattern towards the centre. Other shapes can be filled with couching in a similar manner.

Couching cords and braid

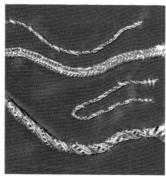

Heavy threads are usually couched singly, and care should be taken to prevent them from unravelling. A pair of pliers is useful for helping to take the thread through to the back of the work. Cords are couched with a diagonal stitch concealed between the twist of the cord. The end of the braid is taken through to the back of the material with a heavy needle. Flat braids, such as Russia braid, are stitched with running stitches down the centre.

Couching plate

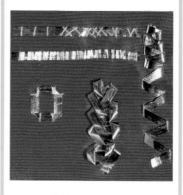

Plate can be attached in straight lines or folded back and forth to form a zigzag pattern. To start and finish, fold back the ends and secure with a double stitch under the fold. For a crimped effect, lay a piece of plate along the length of a large-thread screw and press with your fingernail between the threads to form indentations in the plate.

Couching pearl purl

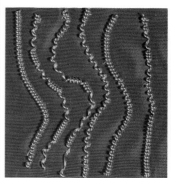

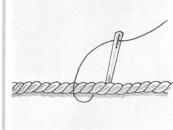

The effect of pearl purl can be varied by pulling out the coils to different thicknesses. It is couched in a similar way to cord, with an invisible diagonal stitch between the twists. In this case the pearl purl is cut to the exact length required and the ends remain on the surface of the fabric, with a double stitch holding them firm.

OR NUÉ

Or nué, also known as shaded gold or Italian shading, is an ancient technique involving the couching of metal threads with fine coloured threads to produce shaded patterns or images. The laid threads cover the entire surface of the design – or that of the area to be worked in or nué.

A smooth, shiny thread such as Jap gold is best, and should be couched with a fine silk or cotton thread which will not cause the laid threads to part. The spacing of the couching stitches is varied to show different amounts of gold thread shining through. It is usual to couch the metal threads in straight lines across the design, which has been painted onto the background fabric. For a freestyle approach, experiments can be made with wavy lines or circular motifs incorporated into a goldwork design which uses other couching techniques.

Preparation

Transfer the design to the background fabric, and colour in the details with fabric paint. As with all types of metal thread embroidery it is essential to frame the work as taut as possible.

▼ **Glenys Grimwood**
Larkspur
A contemporary or nué design worked in coloured silks.

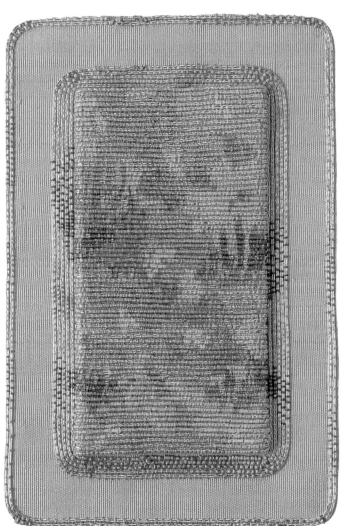

Couching

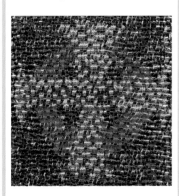

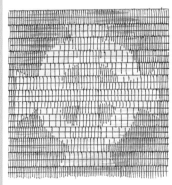

Pairs of metal threads are couched horizontally across the design, starting at the top left-hand corner. A gold-coloured thread is used for couching the background, while coloured threads chosen to match the colours in the design are used for the other areas. Couching is usually worked in a brick pattern, but the spacing of the stitches can vary, allowing you to achieve dense areas of colour which will contrast with the shimmering effect of the gold showing between the couching.

RAISED EFFECTS

Adding texture to an embroidery design always gives an extra dimension. In the case of metal thread embroidery, this can be achieved by padding, and by the application of purls, beads (page 79) and jewels.

Sparkling metallic-effect fabrics can be stitched over a padding of *layers of felt*, as for other types of appliqué (page 88). Gold and silver kid, which is extremely lustrous and should only be used in small quantities, can also be padded with felt.

String which has been dyed yellow can be couched in lines or other patterns and used as a basis for the application of fine cords such as Jap gold.

Small pieces of thin coloured *cardboard* can also be stitched to the surface ready to be covered with lines of couched threads.

Purls come in several sizes and three different qualities: smooth, which is very shiny; rough, which is matt; and check, which is textured. They can be cut into lengths and stitched in a similar way to beads, and because they are flexible they can be formed into loops or stitched over a padding of string.

Basket stitch couching

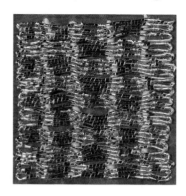

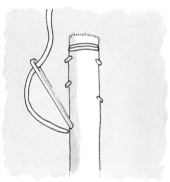

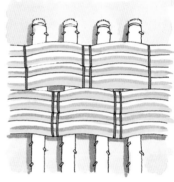

1 Lay a foundation of several lengths of yellow string, securing them to the background fabric with small stitches along the length and a double stitch at either end.

2 For the first row, start at the left, and couch pairs of threads at right-angles to the foundation of string. Work a double couching stitch to the left of the first string, take the metal threads over two strings and work a double stitch to the right of the second string. Repeat with a double stitch before the third string and after the fourth, and so on to the last string.

3 For the second row, repeat this couching method exactly so that four threads are laid together.

4 The third and fourth rows are couched in a similar way to rows one and two, but the thread is secured over one string only at the left-hand side, then couched over two strings as before, so that the flat areas alternate with the raised areas of the previous rows.

Padding with card

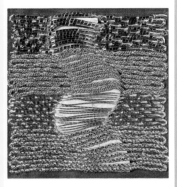

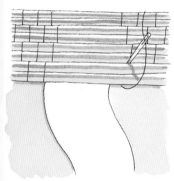

To add texture to an otherwise flat area of couching, small shapes of card or thick craft interfacing can be used as padding. Tack these to the background and work horizontal lines of couched threads to cover them and the surrounding area, with the couching stitches forming an outline around the shape.

Attaching purls

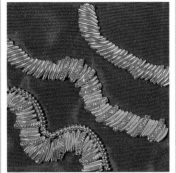

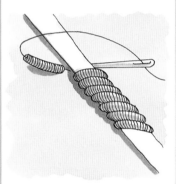

Couch a foundation length of string, securing it firmly at either end with a double stitch. Cut short lengths of purl, but long enough to cover the string at a slight angle. Use a beading needle and a fine thread which has been drawn through a block of beeswax to strengthen it. Stitch the pieces of purl diagonally over the string foundation.

Purls as beads and loops

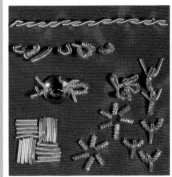

Different types of purls can be cut into varying lengths and stitched to form patterns, textures or decorative motifs. To make loops, a length of purl is threaded onto the beading needle and the needle taken through to the back close to where it originally emerged.

Jewels, beads and sequins

Flat-backed coloured glass jewels and stones are suitable for creating a focal point in a design. Some have holes through which they can be attached. Others can be held in place as for shisha glass (page 109), covered with a mesh of lurex net, or encircled in a ring of leather.

▼ **Pauline Brown**
King's Head
A variety of threads and techniques are combined here with appliquéd fabric and leather, plus trapunto quilting to depict the face.

MACHINE EMBROIDERY

USING THE PRESSER FOOT

FREE MACHINING

TENSIONS

DISSOLVABLE FABRICS

The sewing machine has come a long way since its invention in the 19th century – nowadays modern automatic, electronic and computerized machines provide a wealth of ready-made embroidery stitches and patterns.

The sewing machine can also, of course, be used as a replacement for hand stitching for techniques such as appliqué, quilting, cutwork, etc. In addition, creative and inventive free-style machine embroidery can be produced with an ordinary sewing machine, provided it has a drop-feed and zigzag facility.

It is essential to get to know the finer points of your sewing machine and master the ordinary stitching techniques – once you have done this you can embark on creative work with confidence. Some techniques may require adjustment of the tension. For normal stitching the top and bottom threads should be equally tensioned, producing an even stitch with the top and bottom threads linked precisely, but this is not always necessary for embroidery stitches.

Fabrics

For machine embroidery with the foot on, most types of fabric are suitable, although those which stretch easily need careful handling. For free machining (page 84), firm fabrics such as calico or poplin are easiest for the beginner.

Stitching through an additional backing fabric, which acts as a support, will prevent puckering, particularly for light fabrics.

Threads

Most types of sewing cotton can be used, but machine embroidery threads now include shaded and metallics, which greatly increase the possibilities. For additional texture, various types of cord, as well as knitting, crochet and hand embroidery threads, can be couched by machine.

Needles

Machine needles come in sizes from 120 (heavy) to 70 (very fine). The average sizes, 90 and 100, are best for embroidery. Also available are twin and triple needles for parallel lines, and hem stitch and double hem stitch needles.

Designs

The thin line which straight machine stitching produces gives a delicate spidery effect which can result in rather weak designs. However, the stitching can be built up, overlapped and massed to form close textures, which can produce exciting effects.

Some embroiderers like to work freehand without marking the design on the fabric. However, a few lightly marked guidelines will give you confidence to make a start.

If you prefer a more precise approach, the reversed design, drawn on thin tracing or greaseproof paper can be tacked to the back of the fabric and the main outlines stitched through the paper which is then torn away (page 11).

Straight stitching

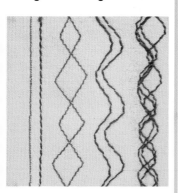

Thread the machine and insert the bobbin in the normal way. Using the standard or the embroidery presser foot, experiment with different types of thread and different stitch lengths. Work stitches in spaced or overlapping rows or mass lines of stitchery to cover the background surface.

Zigzag and satin stitches

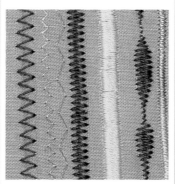

By adjusting the stitch width dial, various widths of stitch can be achieved. This is used in conjunction with the stitch length dial. For example a wide satin stitch requires the highest number stitch width and the lowest stitch length. Experiment with different widths and lengths.

Automatic stitches

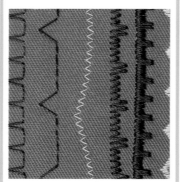

Prepare the machine as for zigzag stitching with a wide stitch width and a low number stitch length. Select an automatic embroidery stitch, test on scrap fabric for effect and then proceed, using a variety of decorative stitches in rows.

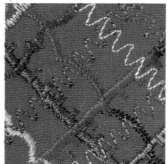

Experiment with different types of thread, and vary the length and width of the stitches.

◀ **Pauline Brown**
Sampler of automatic stitches in shaded threads, securing bands of coloured satins.

USING THE PRESSER FOOT

The most important of the built-in functions of a modern sewing machines is the zigzag facility, which means you can produce automatic embroidery stitches as well as lines of satin stitch.

The range of effects can be extended by attaching different types of presser feet. Most sewing machines have, in addition to the one used for normal stitching, a number of presser feet as standard accessories, while others can be obtained. There are feet for appliqué and quilting; a braiding foot which enables you automatically to couch down braids, cords and heavy yarns; the darning foot, which is for free machining with the feed dogs lowered; and a grooved pin-tucking foot used in combination with twin and triple needles. An interesting looped effect can be produced with the tailor-tacking attachment.

Using the machine with a presser foot means that the fabric is automatically fed through, restricting the stitching to straight or wavy lines – unless the foot is continuously lifted and the work turned.

Hem stitch needles

Use fine crisp fabrics such as organdie or cotton. The single hem stitch needle pierces holes in the fabric. Set the stitch width to 2 and the length to 1.

The double needle uses two top threads and produces a line of straight or zigzag stitches plus the pierced holes. Set the stitch width to 0–2 and length 2. When working several rows, one needle normally pierces the holes in the previous row.

Twin and triple needles

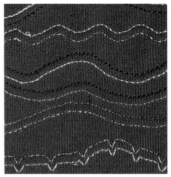

Insert the needle and attach the appropriate pin-tucking foot to produce parallel lines of stitchery. For an Italian quilted or trapunto effect (page 103) thread a thick yarn through the stitching on the back of the work.

Tacking foot

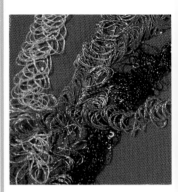

Attach the tailor tacking foot and set the stitch width to 4 and the stitch length to 1. As the stitching proceeds a line of loops is produced which slip off the foot, leaving a raised pile. Closely worked rows are effective if shaded thread is used.

Braiding foot

Wrapped cords

Textures and Patterns

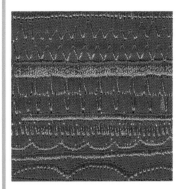 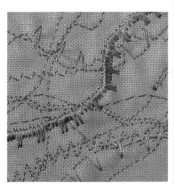

To couch cords, wool or heavy threads automatically onto the background fabric, attach the foot and thread the cord through the hole and under the foot. Set the stitch width to the same width as the cord and adjust the stitch length to your liking. Experiment with different cords, braids and yarns and with some of the automatic embroidery stitches.

The braiding foot can also be used for wrapping threads and cords for additional decoration or finishing touches. Set up the machine as usual, but without a background fabric. Ease the cord through as the stitching proceeds, so that it is wrapped by the machine threads.

Formal patterns and textures can be built up using automatic embroidery stitches.

For a more random approach the work has to be turned frequently and the stitch width altered.

Experimental stitches
Simple geometric and linear designs can be built up and rows of stitches can be massed or overlapped to form areas of texture and colour. As with all experimental work, practice is necessary, but there is much enjoyment to be had, particularly if you try out different fabrics and threads.

◀ **Pauline Brown**
This sample shows the use of various types of presser foot. The fluffy effect of the foliage is achieved with shaded thread and the tacking foot. The braiding foot is used to apply the cords in the foreground and for the wrapped cords of the bush. Twin needle stitching creates the parallel lines of the field.

FREE MACHINING

Free machining, which is often compared to drawing with needle and thread, enables you to use the sewing machine creatively.

There are two methods: one uses the darning foot, and the other is done by removing the presser foot altogether. This means that the fabric is not fed automatically but can be moved around by hand beneath the needle in any direction.

Both methods have their advantages, and it is up to individual embroiderers to decide which they prefer. In both cases the feed dogs have to be disengaged. This is done by using the appropriate switch or button, or on older models, a cover plate is attached.

When free machining without the darning foot, it is essential to mount the fabric in a frame. Choose a shallow round wooden or metal embroidery hoop about 15 cm (6 in) or 20 cm (8 in) in diameter. It should have a screw for adjustment, and the inner ring must be bound with tape so that when the fabric is mounted it is held firmly in place in both directions. A bound frame is less

likely to mark previously worked areas should it be necessary to move to another part of the fabric. The inner ring should stand slightly proud of the other one so that the bottom surface comes directly into contact with the flat bed of the machine – the design will be uppermost on the inside of the ring.

If you prefer not to use a frame, you can work in a similar way by attaching a darning foot and lowering the feed and presser bar. Although it is a little more difficult to see exactly where the needle is piercing the fabric, this method has the advantage of allowing you to embroider larger areas without the need to move a frame.

Stitching

The machine is threaded in the normal way and the bobbin inserted. Whether you are using a darning foot or a frame, the length of the stitch is determined by how fast or slow the work is moved under the needle.

Machine embroidery with straight stitching tends to look thin and tentative unless the stitches are worked close together or overlapped to build up texture and form. If the machine is set to zigzag, the effect will be a wider line which will cover the ground more quickly.

Tensions

Most modern machines have an automatic tension adjustment for ordinary stitching, but it is necessary to alter the normal tension for some decorative effects

and when using different types of thread either on top or in the bobbin.

The top tension is usually numbered on a dial at the front of the machine, which is simply moved to make an adjustment; the bottom tension can be changed by gently turning the screw on the bobbin case. This should be done very carefully to avoid the screw becoming detached completely.

In each case a certain amount of experimentation will be needed to get the correct relationship between the top and bottom tensions. For experiments, use contrasting colours for top and bobbin threads, as this will enable you to check the tension.

Using a frame

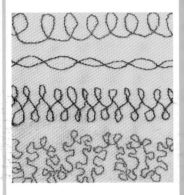

Disengage the feed dogs and set the stitch width and length to 0. Remove the presser foot and position the dressed frame. Lower the presser bar and bring both threads to the surface of the fabric. These are trimmed when several stitches have been worked. Rest your fingers on the edge of the frame and begin to stitch, maintaining a fairly fast speed while moving the frame smoothly in any direction.

Using a darning foot

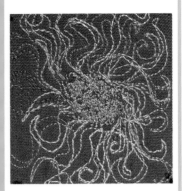

Attach the darning foot, and set up the machine as for free machining with a frame. Do not forget to lower the feed dogs. Stitch in the usual way, moving the fabric back and forth to create the design.

Free zigzag

Set the stitch width to 4 and work free machining as for straight stitching. Satin stitch dots can be worked by zigzagging on the spot.

Whip stitch

This produces a corded line with the lower thread whipping and completely covering the top thread. Use a firm sewing cotton on top and a fine machine embroidery thread in the bobbin. Tighten the top tension and only adjust the bottom tension if necessary. Machine fast and move the frame slowly.

Cable stitch

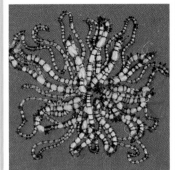

A thick texture using threads such as pearl cotton, knitting yarn or hand embroidery threads can be achieved by working on the reverse side of the fabric. The thick thread is wound by hand on to the bobbin and a thinner one used on top. Loosen the bottom tension so that the thread runs fairly smoothly, and adjust the top tension if necessary.

◄ **Pamela Rooke**
Appliqué and free machining make an effective combination in this underwater scene.

DISSOLVABLE FABRICS

In recent years the production of "vanishing" fabrics has facilitated a technique which simulates lace and can be used as a fabric for garments or accessories. It is worked using free straight stitch machining.

Originally, vanishing muslin and acetone were used for this type of lacy construction, but these have now been superseded by hot- and cold-water dissolvable fabrics.

Whole structures or areas of lacy fabric can be made for wallhangings and other decorative pieces, while lacy edgings and inserts can be fashioned by tacking a fabric on to the dissolvable fabric and heavily stitching along and over the edge.

The method is also suitable for freestanding motifs such as flowers and butterflies. These can be moulded into shape before they are dried, and then either stitched to a background or used on their own as three-dimensional pieces.

Pretty, delicate effects can be achieved with metallic and shaded threads, which can be placed either on top or in the bobbin.

Hot water dissolvable fabric is a fine woven pale blue material which can easily be stretched in a frame. When the embroidery has been completed, it is placed in a pot of boiling water for a few minutes, which causes the fabric to shrivel up and dissolve. To dry and re-shape the lace, it should be pinned out on a towel – or alternatively tacked to a piece of calico before immersion.

Cold water dissolvable fabric resembles a soft, white stretchy plastic. It dissolves very easily in cold water and it does not shrivel up in the same way as the hot-water type. Its only drawback is that it tends to tear. Should this happen an additional piece of the fabric can be placed beneath the hole.

◄ Pamela Rooke
Irises
Machine lace flowers have been embroidered on fabric that is dissolvable in cold water. Fine wire holds the petals in shape.

Outlining the design

Set up the machine for free machining (page 84) with the stitch length and width set to 0. Use machine embroidery threads throughout. Trace the design onto the dissolvable fabric and mount it in a frame. Work free machining over the outlines of the design several times, making sure that the lines overlap and interweave, as otherwise the lace will not hold together.

Filling in the design

To make a pattern within the shape, build up a network of lines which interconnect with each other and the outlines. Machine each line several times, overlapping as for the outline. For a solid effect, the whole shape needs to be filled in with stitches worked in several directions.

Dissolving hot-water fabric

When the stitchery is complete, cut away as much of the dissolvable fabric as

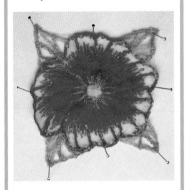

possible before immersing it for a few minutes in a pan of gently simmering water. Rinse with warm water under the tap.

Dissolving cold-water fabric

Cut away the excess fabric as previously, before plunging the embroidery into cold water.

Stretching and drying

Lay the lace on a towel to dry. If it has become distorted, stretch and reshape it, and if necessary pin it in place to dry.

Moulding

For three-dimensional pieces, the lace can be pulled and moulded into shape. This is made easier if it is only immersed for a short time so that some of the dissolvable fabric is left between the machine stitching. For added stiffness, spray-on starch or roller blind stiffener can be used.

APPLIQUÉ

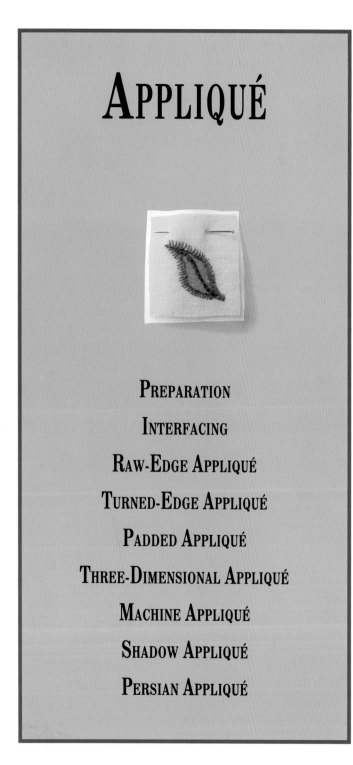

PREPARATION

INTERFACING

RAW-EDGE APPLIQUÉ

TURNED-EDGE APPLIQUÉ

PADDED APPLIQUÉ

THREE-DIMENSIONAL APPLIQUÉ

MACHINE APPLIQUÉ

SHADOW APPLIQUÉ

PERSIAN APPLIQUÉ

The basis of appliqué is the stitching of cut-out designs of different fabrics to a background to create a decorative effect. The method can be used for anything from a simple motif on a bag or T-shirt to a fabric picture, or a full-scale quilt. Falling into the same category of appliqué would be highly textured wallhangings or even three-dimensional forms which use fabrics creatively.

One of the advantages of appliqué is that it is relatively quick to do. Although it was in the past worked by hand, nowadays many people prefer to use the sewing machine for speedy results.

The traditional methods of applying bold shapes to a background are now often adapted, extended or modified, with padded and three-dimensional effects being very popular. Transparent fabrics come into their own in shadow appliqué and even paper and plastic are sometimes featured in contemporary work.

Appliqué can also be used in combination with other embroidery techniques, particularly quilting and surface stitchery, which help to bring out the design in different ways.

Fabrics
Almost any fabric is suitable for appliqué – your choice will depend on the project's use as well as its visual impact. Fabrics such as felt and leather, which do not fray, can be applied direct without turnings. Those which do fray, such as silk, linen, synthetics and cotton, are usually stitched with a turned edge, although today's embroiderers sometimes prefer to exploit the qualities of raw edges, or use a bonding web to apply the fabrics direct.

Although appliqué pieces were not backed in the past, iron-on interfacings and bonding web are often used and are suitable for some methods. For hand appliqué it is advisable to frame the background fabric.

Needles
Any embroidery needle which suits the appliqué fabric can be used. Leather needles are useful for applying leather and plastic, and circular needles for some three-dimensional work.

Designs
In general terms, designs for appliqué are usually fairly bold – often the shapes are simplified, which makes appliqué an ideal method for children's wear or sports-wear. A more sophisticated approach, however, might include more intricate shapes which can be applied with bonding web. Subject matter can be realistic or abstract, with colour and texture being stressed.

PREPARATION

Each appliqué technique requires preparation, and the cutting out and positioning of the fabric pieces must be planned with care. If a design has been drawn up to the correct size, this can be traced to make a paper template for each piece. Sometimes the complete design is drawn onto or transferred to the background fabric ready for the appropriate appliqué pieces to be stitched in place, but this is not always necessary – the cut-out shapes can often be positioned by eye, using the drawn design as a guide.

If a design is to be placed centrally, the centre of both the design and the background fabric should be determined by folding them into quarters and marking the horizontal and vertical lines. These are then aligned when the design is placed on the fabric ready for transferring or the appliqué motif is being positioned.

Preparing paper templates

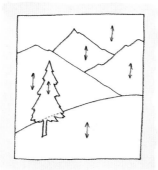

Make a tracing of the design on tracing paper, numbering each shape if necessary. Mark the vertical alignment of each piece with an arrow, so that you can cut each shape on the straight grain of the fabric. Cut out each shape, ready to use according to the chosen appliqué method ie with or without seam allowances.

Order of assembly

The prepared appliqué shapes must be applied in a logical order, overlappng as necessary. Start with the background and gradually superimpose the foreground pieces. It is usually better to overlap shapes rather than try to insert intricate pieces.

▼ **Rose Verney**
Hand-stitched appliquéd cushion, showing the turned edge method. The edge is secured with running stitch.

INTERFACING

In traditional appliqué methods interfacings were of course not used, but many modern embroiderers find them invaluable for some types of appliqué.

Iron-on interfacing, available in a wide range of thicknesses and qualities, is useful for turned-edge appliqué. It not only adds weight and body to the fabric pieces, but also helps to determine their finished size and shape. A bold, stiff effect can be achieved by using heavy craft interfacing, while a softer treatment might involve jersey or flimsy fabrics backed with a lighter-weight interfacing.

Bonding web, which is a paper-backed double-sided adhesive web, can be used for machine appliqué (page 96), Persian appliqué (page 99) and for intricately shaped pieces which could otherwise not be used. It gives an immaculate result with most fabrics and can also be used to bond together different materials. These can then be cut out and used as freestanding motifs.

Interfacing: preparation

Place the interfacing adhesive side up over the design and trace with a hard pencil or fabric marker. Mark the grain line and the pattern number on the non-adhesive side. Cut out the shape carefully and place it adhesive side down on the reverse side of the fabric, aligning the grain if necessary. Press with a steam iron set to the correct heat setting for the fabric.

Interfacing: cutting out

For turned-edge appliqué cut outside the shape, leaving a seam allowance of between 6 mm and 12 mm (¼ in and ½ in), depending on the size and shape of the pieces and the type of fabric. Turn the seam allowances over the edge of the interfacing and tack them in place.

If the interfacing is being used simply to strengthen the fabric for raw-edge appliqué, cut out the shape without turnings.

Interfacing: appliqué

Pin and tack the prepared appliqué in place on the background fabric and stitch in place (see pages 92–3).

Bonding web: preparation

Position the bonding web smooth (non-adhesive) side up over the reverse side of the design tracing. If you are using a template, place this with the wrong side up on the smooth side of the bonding web. Trace the outline, making a reverse image of the pattern piece. Mark the grain line and pattern number on the smooth side.

Cut out the shape, allowing a margin all round. Position this adhesive side down on the reverse side of the fabric, matching grain lines if necessary, and press with an iron set to the appropriate heat setting.

Bonding web: cutting out

Cut out the shape on the marked lines through both the backing paper and the fabric.

Bonding the appliqué

Peel off the backing and iron the shape in place onto the background fabric.

▼ **Anna Christy**
Indian Bedspread and Bird Still Life (detail)
Hand-coloured silks and muslins, stitched with raw edges showing.

TURNED-EDGE APPLIQUÉ

This is the best known of all hand appliqué methods, generally used for appliqué quilts, for fabrics which fray and for padded appliqué. The pieces are cut out with a seam allowance and if desired can be backed with interfacing cut to the finished size. The seam allowances are then turned over and tacked, and the prepared shapes stitched to the background, which can be done in a variety of different ways.

Slip stitch is unobtrusive, particularly if you use thread that matches the appliqué fabric. Stab stitch is more decorative, and can be worked to give an evenly spaced dotted line. Buttonhole stitch (page 20) is also decorative, but may become overbearing. Use it with discretion making tiny stitches which do not impose themselves too much on the design. A variety of other surface stitches can be used either to soften or accentuate the outline.

Marking and cutting out

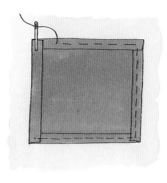

If you are using iron-on interfacing (see page 90), iron this onto the reverse side of the fabric before cutting out. If not, mark the shape on the back of the fabric by drawing round a template or pin the cut-out tracing right side down on the back of the fabric. Cut around the drawn line or round the tracing, allowing a seam allowance of between 6 mm and 12 mm (¼ in and ½ in).

Preparation

Fold over the seam allowance to the reverse side; snip, notch or trim the allowances as necessary, and stitch them down.

Stitching

Frame the background fabric on which the design has been marked. Pin and tack the prepared shape in place, smoothing any folds.

Slip stitch along the edge by bringing the needle up through the background fabric close to the edge of the motif and taking a tiny stitch into the turned edge. Remove the tacking stitches.

Decorative stitches

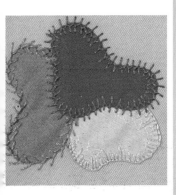

Cretan, feather and buttonhole stitch are all suitable for embellishing and covering the edges of applied fabrics.

Curves

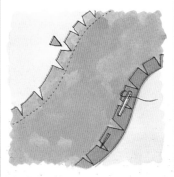

If interfacing is not being used it may be helpful to machine stitch a line of stay-stitching on the fold line. For inward curves, snip the seam allowance at regular intervals to within 3 mm (⅛ in) of the interfacing or stay-stitching. For outward curves, remove small notches of fabric from the seam allowance to reduce the excess bulk. Snip to within 3 mm (⅛ in) as for inward curves. Fold over the seam allowance and tack it in place.

▶ **Jill Cotton**
Letter S
Felt appliqué, some pieces being overlaid with net.

Points and corners

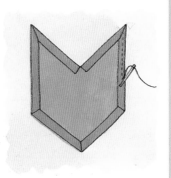

At outer corners and acute angles, trim the seam allowance to reduce bulk. Fold down the point first, then the two sides. On inner corners, snip the fabric up to the stay-stitching or the interfacing and turn back the sides. Tack in place ready for attaching.

RAW-EDGE APPLIQUÉ

Non-woven fabrics such as felt, net and leather can all be cut out and applied directly without a seam allowance, either by machine or with stab or slip stitch.

Experimental decorative panels often include fabrics which have been cut out and randomly applied, with the raw edges creating a design feature. For a textured or impressionistic effect, tiny pieces of a variety of materials can be tacked or glued in position prior to stitching by hand or machine.

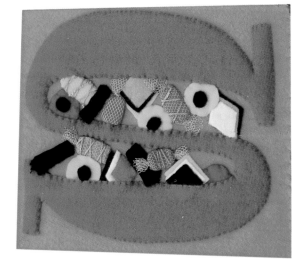

PADDED APPLIQUÉ

Appliqué can be used in combination with a variety of different padding materials to create textured and raised areas. If the appliqué is non-woven, such as felt or leather, it is applied with raw edges on top of the padding, but for most other types of fabric the turned-edge method must be used.

The kind of padding you use depends both on the use to which the article will be put and on the effect you are seeking. Traditionally layers of felt were used. These are particularly suitable for padding suede and leather or for areas of a design where a firmness is needed. Synthetic wadding produces a softer effect, and enables you to work embroidery through it on the raised area. Card or craft interfacing gives a stiffer, more precise result, and is ideal for hard-edged subjects such as architectural or geometric designs.

Padding with felt

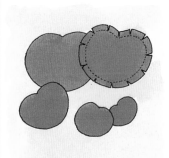

Cut out a piece of felt the same size and shape as the appliqué motif, then cut several more shapes, each slightly smaller than the previous one.

Starting with the smallest, pin and stitch it in the centre of the area to be padded, using a stab stitch worked at right-angles to the edge of the felt. Stitch the next size on top and repeat until each piece is attached, then sew down the prepared appliqué shape.

Padding with wadding

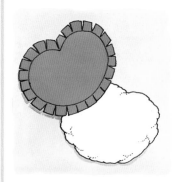

Cut a piece of wadding the same shape and size as the prepared appliqué shape. Stitch the wadding to the background with loose straight stitches at right-angles to the edge. Stitch the appliqué shape on top.

Card or craft interfacing

Cut the card or stiff interfacing to the size and shape of the finished appliqué motif. Cut out the fabric with a seam allowance. Centre the card on the reverse side of the fabric and apply fabric glue sparingly. Fold the fabric over the edge. Alternatively, use bonding web, ironing the seam allowance over the edge. Slip stitch the appliqué to the background.

THREE-DIMENSIONAL APPLIQUÉ

A popular method today, taking the theme of padded appliqué a step further, is the production of small free-standing motifs such as leaves and flowers, which are then stitched in place on embroidered or appliqué panels, boxes or even garments.

Flat, raw-edged shapes can be made with two layers of fabric bonded together. If the motif needs to be manipulated into shape, florists' wire can be placed between the fabrics before bonding. A stiffened effect can be achieved by spraying with roller-blind stiffener, or applying a weak solution of fabric adhesive.

Padded shapes, with either raw or turned edges, can be stuffed with wadding, and the edges and details embroidered either by hand or machine.

Flat bonded motifs

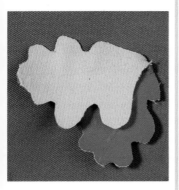

Using bonding web, adhere two fabrics together with the right sides out. Mark the design and cut out. The edges can be left unadorned or decorative stitches and details can be added.

Padded raw-edged motifs

Mark the shape on the top fabric. Place this on the bottom fabric with a layer of wadding between. Tack the layers together lightly and machine stitch (or back stitch by hand) along the marked outline. Cut out the motif close to the stitching and work machine satin or zigzag (or close buttonhole by hand).

Turned-edge motifs

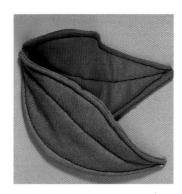

1 Mark the shape on the reverse side of the top fabric. Place the top and bottom fabrics right sides together with the wadding beneath. Tack them together, then machine stitch along the marked outline. Cut a diagonal slit in the bottom fabric. This will be used for turning the work. Remove the tacking, cut out the motif and trim the wadding fairly close to the stitching.

2 Turn the motif through to the right side. Press lightly and stitch up the opening. Finish by top stitching the edge and details by machine, or add decorative edging by hand.

MACHINE APPLIQUÉ

Machine appliqué has the advantage of speed as well as producing an immaculate effect. It stands up well to hard wear or frequent washing.

In machine appliqué the edges are usually crisply defined, and satin stitch is often used to make a bold outline. A sewing machine which has the facility for zigzag stitching is useful – some have a special transparent appliqué foot which enables you to see exactly where the needle pierces the fabric.

Although straight stitching can be used in conjunction with turned-edge appliqué, it is most usual to apply fabrics with raw edges. These can either be bonded or tacked in place, and the edges are then concealed beneath an outline of zigzag or satin stitch. The stitch-and-cut method is good for small pieces of appliqué. Automatic machine embroidery stitches give a decorative effect ideal for simple shapes, but for a less formal approach free machining can soften edges or produce additional colour, texture or pattern around a motif.

Bond and stitch

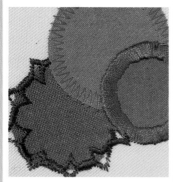

Fix the appliqué motif to the background fabric using bonding web (page 90 or 91). Attach the appliqué presser foot to the sewing machine, set the stitch width and length to your chosen setting, and cover the edges with stitching.

Stitch and cut

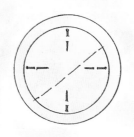

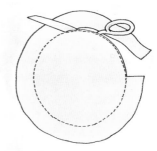

Mark and cut out the motif to be applied, leaving a margin all round. Pin (and tack if necessary) in place on the background fabric, making sure that it lies smoothly. Work straight machine stitches around the marked outline and then carefully cut away the excess fabric. If you wish, the edge can be covered with zigzag, satin or decorative embroidery stitches.

Zigzag and satin stitch

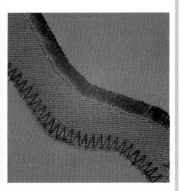

Keeping the appliqué to the left of the needle, stitch in a clockwise direction round the motif so that the right-hand edge of the zigzag pierces the background fabric.

Zigzagging outside corners

Work zigzag or satin stitch to the corner, stopping the machine with the needle to the right. Keep the needle in the fabric and pivot the work, continuing stitching along the next side.

Zigzagging inside corners

Work in a similar way as for outside corners, but stop the machine with the needle to the left. Pivot and continue stitching.

Acute points and corners

The zigzag stitch can be tapered by gradually narrowing the stitch towards the corner. Pivot the work as usual and stitch the other side, gradually increasing the stitch width.

Free machining

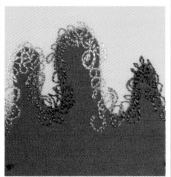

Bond or tack the appliqué motif in place. Mount the work in a frame and work free straight or zigzag machining (page 81) over the edges.

▶ **Greta Fitchett**
Apples
Silk, satins and sheer fabrics have been appliquéd with satin and zigzag stitching.

SHADOW APPLIQUÉ

The delicate effect of transparent fabrics such as organdie, organza and voile, used in a variation of the stitch-and-cut method (page 96) produces the technique known as shadow appliqué. In this case the fabric to be applied is placed beneath the transparent background fabric, to provide the "shadow", and the excess is cut away after stitching.

Originally a hand method, sewn with pin stitch, shadow appliqué is now usually worked by machine using a narrow zigzag stitch. Traditionally only white fabrics were used, both for the appliqué and the main fabric, but it is possible to experiment with different types of coloured fabric.

The soft effects which are a feature of this technique make it a suitable medium for lingerie or evening wear. Designs should be fairly simple in concept, with clearly defined areas, rather like a stencil, so that the excess fabric can be easily removed.

Preparation

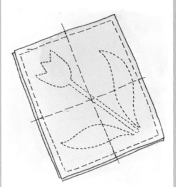

Trace the design onto the transparent fabric. For the appliqué, cut sufficient fabric to cover the whole design area and tack it onto the underside of the top fabric, making sure that the grains of both fabrics are aligned.

Katharine Guerrier
Here, coloured fabrics have been used for the "shadows" and ornamental chain-stitched detail added through both layers.

Machine stitching

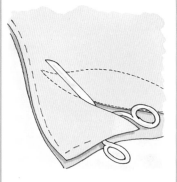

Work straight machine stitching along the marked outline and carefully cut away the excess fabric from the back layer. Finish by covering the edges of the appliqué with zigzag, satin or free machine stitching.

Hand stitching

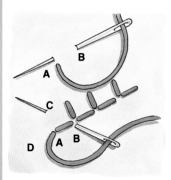

On the right side, work pin stitch through both layers before cutting away the excess fabric from the underneath. To work pin stitch, work a back stitch from A to B along the marked outline and bring the needle up again at A. Repeat the back stitch on top of the first, bringing the needle up at C, inserting it again at A and bringing it up at D. Pull the thread fairly tight to produce small holes in the transparent fabric.

PERSIAN APPLIQUÉ

Persian appliqué, also known as broderie perse, appliqué perse and cretonne appliqué, developed in the 19th century as an inexpensive imitation of embroidery. Motifs such as birds, flowers and animals were cut from printed cretonnes or other fabrics and reassembled on plain-coloured backgrounds.

The pieces are applied with raw edges, and the simplest method is to iron a piece of bonding web to the back of the printed fabric before the motifs are cut out. When they have been positioned and ironed in place, they can be stitched by hand, either with invisible or decorative stitches, or with fancy or zigzag machine stitching.

This is a simple method particularly well suited to the inexperienced designer, as different arrangements of the cut-out shapes can be tried out on the background fabric before ironing down. It is ideal for cushions, quilts and garments, where a quick and easy method is required.

Preparation

Cut out printed motifs with small sharp scissors. If you are using bonding web, this should be ironed on before the motifs are cut out.

Stitching

Arrange the cut-out motifs to form a satisfactory design and either bond or pin and tack them in place on the background fabric. If working by hand mount the work in a frame. Secure the edges with invisible slip stitches (page 92) or decorative hand stitches. Alternatively machine stitch with zigzag, satin or automatic embroidery stitches.

Katharine Guerrier
These flowers have machine-stitched detail added to the basic outline using shaded thread for a more subtle effect.

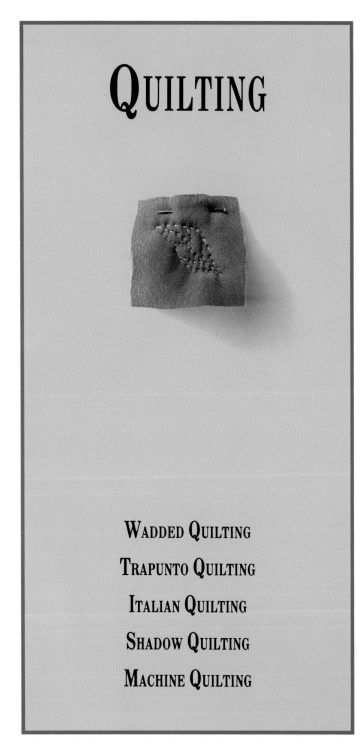

QUILTING

WADDED QUILTING

TRAPUNTO QUILTING

ITALIAN QUILTING

SHADOW QUILTING

MACHINE QUILTING

The origins of quilting are lost in history, but it is known that by the 16th century padded garments were in common use as protection under armour, and silk quilts are often mentioned in the household inventories of the great European estates.

During the past hundred years, the popularity of quilting has increased in Europe and North America, not only for traditional quilts but also for garments, household items and wallhangings.

There are several different quilting techniques, giving very different finished effects. All of them are relatively simple to do, and can be stitched either by hand or by machine.

▼ **Sonja Galsworthy**
Tree forms
Example of wadded quilting, worked on satin with beads added.

Frames
It is advisable to use a frame for most types of hand quilting. The hoops used for quilting, deeper than the normal embroidery hoops, are available in a range of sizes, and are either circular or oval. Large floor-standing models are used by professional quiltmakers, but these take up a great deal of space.

Marking the design
This should be done as lightly as possible and several methods are suitable, including direct tracing (page 10), pricking and pouncing (page 10) or using stencils or templates (page 89).

Stitches for quilting
Back stitch (page 16).
Running stitch (page 15).

WADDED QUILTING

Wadded quilting (also known as English quilting) consists of three layers of fabric, wadding and fabric, tacked and stitched together either by hand or machine.

The Japanese technique of Sashiko, with its dark blue fabric and white hand stitching, is constructed in a similar way.

Fabrics
The top fabric may be any closely woven material, such as cotton, silk or synthetic fibres. The choice of backing fabric depends on whether it will be seen, as it would be on a quilt, or hidden, as on a cushion cover. Synthetic wadding can be washed or dry-cleaned and so is most often used, but silk, wool and cotton waddings (available from specialist quilting shops) give quilting a different character.

Threads
Strong quilting or buttonhole thread gives a clearly defined line.

Needles
Quilting needles (or betweens) are good but any sharp embroidery needle of suitable size can be used.

Templates and stencils

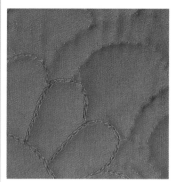

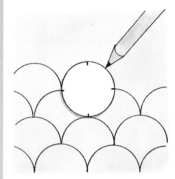

1 Using either of these to mark out repeat designs not only makes this process easier, but is more likely to be accurate. You can either cut your own stencil or template from card or use a purchased one. On templates, either cut out notches or make marks at various points along the edges to make it easier to match up the various parts of the design so that overlapping areas are uniform.

2 Quilting stencils have slits through which the design is marked. This results in broken lines that have to be joined when the stencil is removed. Use a quilter's marker, a water-soluble pen or dressmakers' chalk pen, pressing very lightly.

Tacking

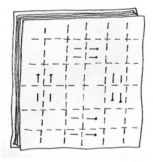

Having transferred the design to the top fabric, place this on top of the wadding which you have aligned carefully with the edges of the backing fabric. Check that the grain lines of top and backing fabric match. Pin the three layers together, smoothing out wrinkles from the centre. Tack in grid formation, about 5 cm (2 in) apart, starting at the centre and working outwards. Now mount the work in a frame (see page 100).

Stitching

To start a thread, make a small knot at the end, bring the needle up through to the right side and tug gently to pull the knot through the backing fabric and into the wadding but no further. To finish off, take the thread through the wadding a short way, bring the needle out through the backing fabric and cut off the thread close to the surface.

When stitching the design, work small, even running stitches along the marked lines, through all three layers. For a solid line, back stitch can be worked, while embroidery stitches such as chain or stem stitch are sometimes used for a decorative effect. When quilting is used in combination with appliqué, the stitches are either made along the edge of the applied motif or a short distance from it, following the shape exactly.

TRAPUNTO QUILTING

Also known as stuffed quilting, this is a decorative method in which the small padded areas stand out in relief against a flat background.

Two layers of fabric are first tacked together, then the motifs to be padded are enclosed with stitching so that they can be stuffed from the reverse side.

Fabrics
The top fabric needs to be pliable to accommodate the stuffing, while the backing should be lightweight but firm. Wadding is usually used to stuff the motifs.

Threads
For decorative work, any embroidery or sewing thread may be used.

Needles
Embroidery needles of suitable sizes are best.

Preparation

Mark the design on the top fabric as for wadded quilting (page 101). Pin and tack the top and backing fabrics together, matching grain lines, and mount the work in a frame (page 100).

Stitching

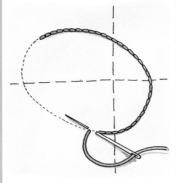

Work back stitch along the outlines of the design so that the motifs to be padded are enclosed.

Stuffing

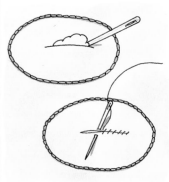

Keeping the work in the frame, turn it over to the wrong side. Taking care not to cut the top fabric, cut a small slit diagonally in the backing fabric within the outline of a shape that is to be stuffed. Insert small pieces of wadding through the slit into the shape. Gently push the wadding into any corners using a blunt implement, such as a knitting or tapestry needle. Check the front of the quilting – you should aim for a smooth, rounded shape – then carefully oversew the edges of the slit together.

◄ **Pauline Brown**
Printed fabric raised to produce a relief effect with trapunto quilting for the main areas and Italian quilting for the outlines. As an alternative to backstitch, chain stitch has been used for a more decorative effect.

ITALIAN QUILTING

Like trapunto quilting this method starts with two layers of fabric, but, in this case, double lines of stitching are worked. Then quilting wool, threaded in a large-eyed needle, is inserted from the back of the work and run between the two layers of fabric and between the lines of stitching.

Fabrics
The top fabric should not be too stiff otherwise the quilting will not show up well. The backing fabric needs to be lightweight but firm.

Threads
The surface stitching is worked in sewing cotton in a colour that matches the background fabric. Quilting wool is used to fill the channels.

Needles
Embroidery needles of suitable sizes are ideal, while a large-eyed wool needle is necessary for inserting the quilting wool.

Preparation

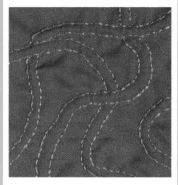

Mark the design on the top fabric as for wadded quilting (page 101). Pin and tack the top and backing fabrics together, matching grain lines, and mount the work in a frame (page 100).

Stitching

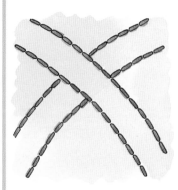

Work parallel lines of back stitch along the marked lines.

▶ **Alison Collie**
Letter A
An interlaced design worked in Italian quilting is combined with a letter worked in padded trapunto quilting.

Insertion

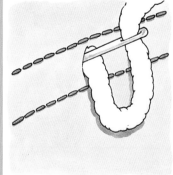

Loosen the tension of the work in the frame just enough to make the surface pliable. Thread the quilting wool into a large-eyed tapestry or wool needle and insert it, from the wrong side, at the beginning of one of the channels and carefully turn it so it is lying between the parallel lines of stitching, pointing along the channels. Slide the needle carefully along the channel and bring it out again through the backing fabric. Re-insert the needle through the same hole to work the next part of the design. To avoid puckering at corners or sharp curves, leave the wool loosely tensioned. Keep a small pair of pliers to hand to pull the needle through.

Shadow Quilting

There are several forms of this attractive method of quilting, but essentially it relies for its effect on the transparent top fabric used in its construction.

The most usual method is for a visible filling, such as coloured felt shapes, to be tacked between the top fabric and the backing, so that the raised shape shows through but is softened by the mistiness of the top fabric.

Shadow Italian quilting is worked in exactly the same way as Italian quilting (page 103), but the colours of the wools inserted in the channels show as delicate shadowy lines through the transparent top layer of fabric.

Trapunto quilting can also be adapted in this way by stuffing areas with strongly coloured wadding or wool.

Fabrics
Shadow quilting relies for its effect on careful choice of fabrics and materials. The backing fabric and inserted materials should be strongly coloured, while pale fabrics in organza, net or chiffon should be used on top.

Threads
Ordinary sewing cotton is used for quilting. Thick knitting, tapestry or quilting wool or coloured wadding are required for the insertions in shadow Italian or trapunto quilting.

Needles
Appropriately sized embroidery needles are needed to work the quilting. For inserting wool, large-eyed wool needles are required.

Visible filling method

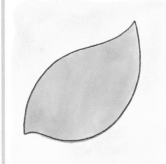

1 Mark the design on the opaque backing fabric and mount this in a frame (pages 100 and 101). Cut out the motif to be applied in felt and tack it lightly in place on the backing, making sure that the knot is underneath and the lines on the backing fabric are covered.

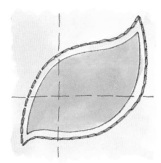

2 Position the transparent top fabric over the work, aligning the grains, then pin and tack it into place. Stitch around the felt motif, with running, back, chain or any decorative line stitch you like.

Combined shadow-work

For the shadow Italian quilting, mark the design on the opaque backing fabric and mount the work in a frame (pages 100 and 101). Position the transparent top fabric over the work, aligning the grains, and pin and tack it into place. Work parallel lines of back stitch along the marked lines, as you would for conventional Italian quilting. To work the quilting, loosen the tension of the work in the frame to make the fabrics a little more supple. Thread the coloured tapestry or quilting wool into a large-eyed tapestry needle and insert the wool between the lines of stitching as for Italian quilting (page 103).

For shadow trapunto quilting, mark the design and prepare the fabrics as for shadow Italian quilting. Work an outline of back stitch around the motif to be stuffed. Insert coloured wools or dyed wadding from the back of the work as you would in conventional trapunto quilting (page 102).

◀ **Mari Yoneyama**
A simple floral motif with cut-out shapes in felt.

MACHINE QUILTING

All quilting techniques may be carried out by machine, though the designs may need to be adapted or simplified.

Some sewing machines have accessories such as quilting guides that are specially designed for machine quilting. Also available is a walking foot attachment. This will glide over even very thick layers of wadding.

As it is not possible to frame up large pieces of fabric and insert them under the arm of the machine, it is particularly important to tack the layers together carefully. In order to prevent distorting the overall shape of the fabric, always stitch in the same direction from top to bottom, starting from the centre of the top edge, then working in the same way towards the sides. For less formal designs, start in the centre of the design and work outwards.

When making up an item that has to be a certain finished size, such as a garment, allow extra fabric as some shrinkage may take place while quilting.

Fabrics
Most fabrics are amenable to being quilted by machine.

Threads
Sewing cotton, buttonhole thread or quilting thread.

Needles
Sizes 90–100 are best.

Designs
Many designs suitable for hand quilting can also be used for machine work, though intricate patterns and motifs that require continual turning of the work are best avoided. Geometric designs and those with gentle curves, however, are straight-forward, and bold or large-scale motifs can easily be stitched by machine.

Quick quilting

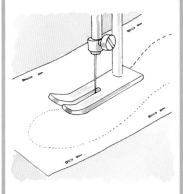

Prepare the layers of fabric and wadding as for hand quilting, working a grid of tacking (page 101). Transfer the design to tracing or greaseproof paper and pin and tack this in position on top of the prepared fabrics.

Set a long stitch length and machine through all layers, following the marked lines on the paper. Start in the centre and gradually work outwards, smoothing the fabric and tracing as you go. Carefully tear away the paper, take the loose threads to the back of the work and finish off.

Using a quilting guide

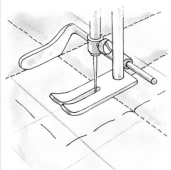

This useful accessory enables you to stitch parallel lines some distance apart and so it is suitable for diaper (diamond), striped and grid patterns of straight or wavy lines.

Always work in the same direction from top to bottom or from the same side to avoid puckering the fabric.

Decorative quilting

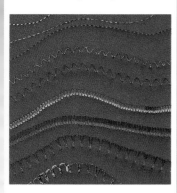

Italian machine quilting

Although machine quilting is usually worked using a straight machine stitch, zigzag and satin stitch can also be used to great effect when more defined lines are required. Automatic embroidery stitches can also be used to produce more decorative effects, particularly on plain fabrics.

Twin needles spaced at either 3 or 4 mm (⅛ or ³⁄₁₆ in) apart are ideal for producing the parallel line designs needed for this method, using either an opaque top fabric or a transparent one for shadow Italian quilting.

▼ **Machine quilting**
Pauline Brown
An example of the decorative effect when different machine stitches are used to quilt a plain fabric.

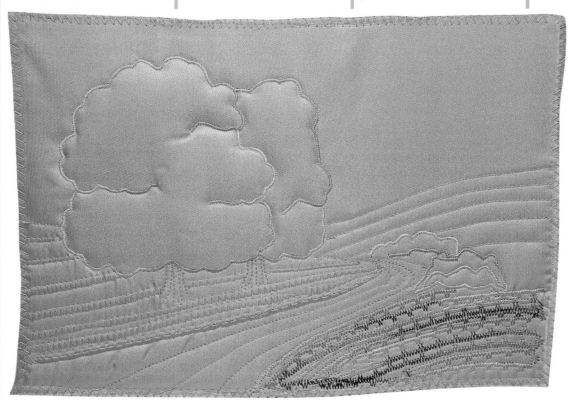

OTHER TECHNIQUES

BEADWORK

CUTWORK

BRODERIE ANGLAISE

NEEDLELACE

NEEDLEWEAVING

NET EMBROIDERY

RIBBON WORK

SHADOW WORK

SMOCKING

REVERSE SMOCKING

STUMPWORK

Besides the more common embroidery techniques, there are a number of other methods which are interesting to try out. They mostly involve the use of familiar stitches, but perhaps combined with another type of fabric or a slightly different method of working.

Beadwork, smocking and ribbon embroidery are mostly used for decorating garments or accessories, but they also are useful for adding texture to an embroidered wall-hanging or panel.

In the past, *cutwork and broderie anglaise embroidery* played a big part in the embellishment of table- and bedlinen. They can still be used for this purpose, but if the openwork aspect of the technique is exploited, new ideas and designs can be developed.

Needlelace and stumpwork are closely related in their use of stitches but the latter employs a number of special methods and materials to create raised effects.

Needleweaving is a versatile technique which can be worked in association with drawn thread work, on a background fabric, or even across an open space. The weaving may be stitched in regular patterns or freely.

The delicacy of *shadow work and net embroidery* appeals to many embroiderers. Although these techniques are limited in their practical use, the transparent fabrics and pretty stitches are ideal for creating small pictures or garments for special occasions.

BEADWORK

Beads produce an interesting textural surface and are also useful for creating or highlighting small details, while sequins, spangles, shisha glass and ''jewels'' add an air of theatricality and glamour.

Fabrics
Beads can be attached to any fabric, though chiffon or voile may need a lightweight backing, such as lawn. Work should be framed for stitching.

Threads
Use a strong thread such as sewing cotton or polyester that is fine enough to pass easily through the hole in the bead or sequin. To further strengthen the thread and prevent it twisting, draw it through a block of beeswax.

Needles
Beading needles are very long and fine. However, they tend to bend – replace them when this happens.

Designs
Beads catch the light and create textures and patterns that will be a dominant feature of a design.

Stitching individual beads

Textures and patterns can be built up with massed beads and sequins sewn on singly. Sequins may be secured with two or three stitches or held in place by sewing a bead in the centre.

Loops and fringes

A number of beads are threaded onto lengths of cotton, formed into loops and the needle inserted close to where it originally emerged. A fringed effect can be made by threading several beads on to the cotton and then taking the needle back through each one except the one at the bottom end.

Stitching in rows

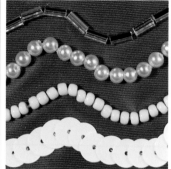

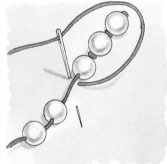

1 Beads, threaded on a length of cotton, are laid on the surface, with a couching thread catching them in place at intervals.

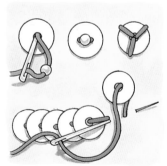

2 Overlapping sequins are each sewn in place with a back stitch, one at a time, in such a way that the stitches are invisible.

Applying shisha glass

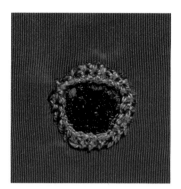

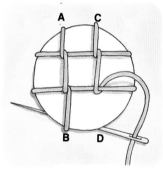

1 Hold the mirror circle firmly in place and make two parallel stitches across the glass. Bring the needle out at A, pass it over and back under the first thread, and then repeat this over and under the second thread. Insert the needle at B, then bring it out at C and repeat the first holding stitch, finishing at D.

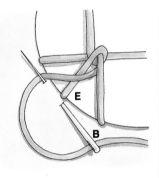

2 For the shisha stitch, bring the needle out at E and take it over the intersecting base threads. make a small stitch alongside the edge of the glass, keeping the thread below the needle. Repeat, taking the thread over the base threads, and working in a clockwise direction around the perimeter of the glass.

CUTWORK

The elaborate cutwork methods of the past are rarely seen today, mainly due to the difficulty and intricacy of the work involved in creating them. However, simple but beautiful cutwork designs can be worked entirely in button-hole stitch with areas of the background cut away to focus the eye on the main motifs. To progress a stage further to Renaissance cutwork, buttonhole bars are added across the spaces. Stitching picots on the bars is the basis of a lacy effect known as Richelieu cutwork.

Fabrics
A good choice is closely woven linen or medium-weight cotton, which will not fray. It is essential to frame up the work to prevent distortion.

Threads
Usually, these are chosen to match the background fabric or can be slightly darker in tone. Coton à broder, stranded cotton or linen thread are most often used.

Needles
Embroidery needles of a suitable size are best.

Designs
In planning a cutwork design, the relationship between the main motifs and the cut-away background areas needs to be considered. Cutwork requires neat stitching and the design should be marked on the fabric with an erasable fabric marker. Mark the areas to be cut with an X.

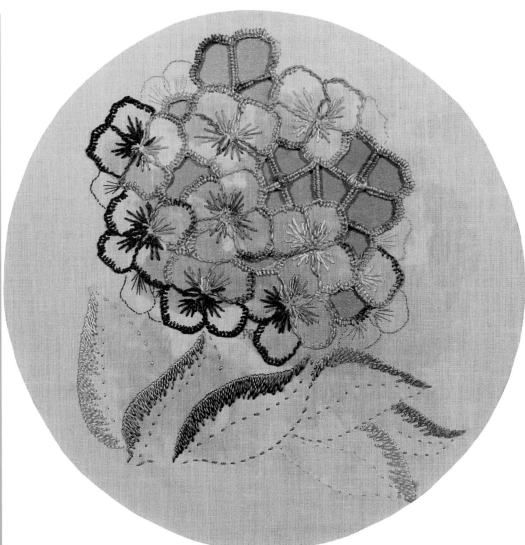

▲ **Pauline Brown**
Hydrangea
Coloured cutwork worked on a painted background.

Simple cutwork

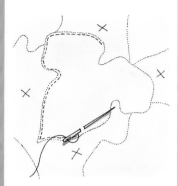

1 Transfer the design (page 110) precisely but lightly to the fabric, marking the areas that will eventually be cut away with an X. Frame the fabric (page 100) and work small running stitches just inside the outlines and slightly away from the marked areas.

Work close, regular buttonhole stitches (page 20) over the running stitch base, placing the loop of the buttonhole stitch nearest to the area to be cut away.

2 When all the stitching has been completed, carefully cut away the background areas as close as possible to the stitching.

Renaissance cutwork

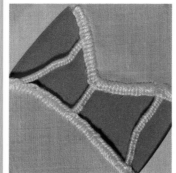

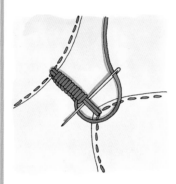

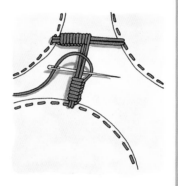

1 To work buttonhole bars, take the thread across the area to be cut away and make a small stitch to fasten it. Repeat this twice, so that three threads lie together in parallel. Work buttonhole stitch over the bar of threads, but not through the fabric. Finish off and then continue outlining the shape with running stitch.

2 To work branched bars, lay the base threads as for buttonhole bars and work buttonhole stitch halfway along the bar. To form the branch, lay three threads from here across to the edge of the cutwork area and work buttonhole stitch along them back to the first bar. Continue working buttonhole stitch along the rest of the first bar to complete it.

Richelieu cutwork

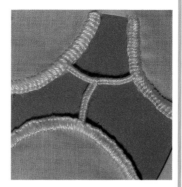

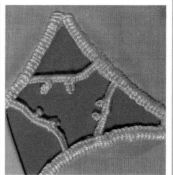

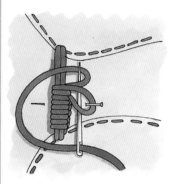

To work looped picots, lay the base threads as for buttonhole bars (page 27) and work buttonhole stitch halfway along the bar. To form the picot, insert a pin through the fabric at right angles to the bar, loop the thread under the pin, from left to right, over the bar and then under the loop. Twist the working thread round the needle before pulling the thread tightly. Remove the pin and continue working buttonhole stitch along the bar.

BRODERIE ANGLAISE

Another cutwork technique, broderie anglaise or eyelet embroidery, came into fashion in the latter half of the 19th century, developing out of the more delicate whitework technique known as Ayrshire embroidery.

Fabrics
Medium-weight cotton or polycotton fabrics that do not fray are ideal. Frame the fabric as you would for cutwork (page 110).

Threads
As for other types of cutwork.

Needles
Fine embroidery needles, plus a stiletto for piercing the holes, are required.

Designs
These differ from simple cutwork designs in that it is the holes rather than the spaces between them that are the main feature. Often floral motifs are made up of eyelet and teardrop shapes. Scalloped edges are the traditional method of finishing.

Broderie anglaise Preparation

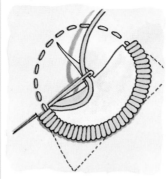

Transfer the design (page 113) and work running stitch round the marked outlines as for cutwork (page 111).

Shaded eyelets
For small shaded eyelets and teardrop shapes (which are overcast with stitches that increase in size to give the original opening an elongated appearance) work a double outline, padding the stitching with lines of running stitch.

Pierced eyelets

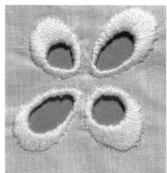

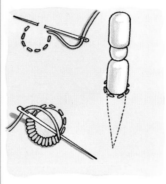

For small pierced eyelets, pierce a hole inside the reinforcing running stitches with a stiletto. Work fine overcast stitches over the edge.

Cut eyelets

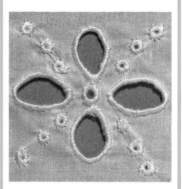

When making large circular and oval cut eyelets and large teardrop shapes, the fabric must be cut. Snip the fabric from the centre of the hole towards the running stitch outline both vertically and horizontally. Turn back the four points to the wrong side and work overcast stitches over the running stitches. Trim away the parts of the points that still protrude from the stitching.

▶ Kathryn Francis
Circular and teardrop overcast eyelets are counterbalanced with simple cutwork areas that give strength to this delicate design.

Scalloped edging

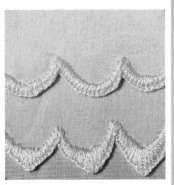

The design for a simple semicircular scallop can be made by using a coin to draw the two outlines about 1 cm (½ in) from the edge of the fabric. Outline both edges with running stitches and pad the area between with more running stitches. Work close buttonhole stitches vertically over the running stitches. When the stitching is complete, trim the excess fabric close to the stitching. Variations in size and design can be used to decorative effect.

NEEDLELACE

Needlelace fillings are networks of delicate stitches that are often incorporated in cutwork (page 111) and drawn thread (page 64) embroidery, when they are usually stitched across the open spaces to give designs more delicacy and interest. They can also be worked as a form of detached embroidery over padding, as in stumpwork (page 124), or stitched free of the background except at the edges, so they are extremely versatile and useful.

Fabrics
Freestanding motifs may be mounted on stiff paper or acetate in order to work them. Needlelace fillings worked on the surface may be stitched on any type of fabric, but it should be framed otherwise it is very easy to pucker the surrounding fabric.

▶ **Pamela Rooke**
Orchid
A three-dimensional, needlelace piece, made on a wired cordonnet, incorporating several different stitches.

Threads
Smooth-textured yarns such as crochet cotton, linen thread, coton à broder or pearl cotton are the most suitable threads. The form of the stitches will be most easily seen when worked in these materials.

Needles
Tapestry needles of suitable size are best as they will not split the threads.

Designs
The technique lends itself to freestyle abstract designs with curved edges. For three-dimensional work, detached buttonhole lace can be manipulated to cover padded areas.

Working on a background

Mark the design on the background (page 10–11), and frame the work (page 100). Outline the shape with small back stitches. This will form a base through which the rows of detached buttonhole fillings are worked. These are attached only by the back stitch outline and do not pass through the fabric, except at the beginning and the end.

Working on a cordonnet

A cordonnet is a continuous double outlining thread that acts as an anchorage for freestanding or unsupported needlelace. Fine wire can also be incorporated to make it easier to maintain the outline for the needlelace. Prepare a temporary foundation of supporting layers of fabric, stiff paper or acetate on which the design has been marked. Couch the cordonnet in place along the outline of the shape to be filled. When the filling stitches have been completed, cut away the couching stitches from the supporting foundation.

Detached buttonhole filling

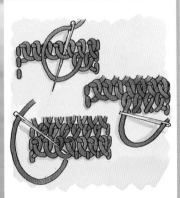

This is formed in a similar way to surface embroidery buttonhole stitch (page 20), using sufficient yarn to complete the stitching. If working on a back stitch outline, work the first row, from left to right, looping the stitch through this and through the back stitch at the end of the row. The second row, worked from right to left, is looped through the first row, and so on. To finish, either loop the last row into the back stitch or background fabric; alternatively stitch each loop down with a small vertical stitch.

When using a cordonnet loop the detached stitches round the cordonnet. On completion, the ends are darned in to the cordonnet.

Straight stitch return

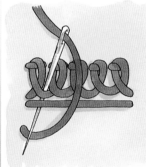

Work the first row of detached buttonhole stitches from left to right, then take the working thread round the outline of back stitches or the cordonnet and return with a straight stitch to the left-hand side.

For the second and subsequent rows, work from left to right, looping the detached buttonhole stitches over the straight stitch return thread as well as the previous row of buttonhole stitches.

This can be worked loosely or to give a firm, solid effect.

Double buttonhole filling

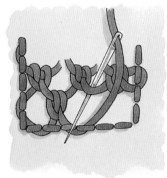

1 Work the first buttonhole stitch into the second outlining back stitch, leaving a loose loop. Then work a second buttonhole stitch into the same back stitch, pulling the thread fairly tight. Continue working pairs of buttonhole stitches into alternate back stitches, leaving loops between the pairs.

2 For the second row, work from right to left, stitching the pairs of buttonhole stitches through the loops of the previous row. A similar but lacier effect can be made with triple groups of buttonhole stitches.

NEEDLEWEAVING

Needleweaving is very often associated with drawn thread work (page 64), but it is also a technique in its own right when worked on the surface or even across an open space or ring. A series of base (warp) threads are laid down alongside one another and these are then woven together to create either spidery forms or solid areas of pattern. Beads, curtain rings and metal discs can all be incorporated on the base threads to give an extra interest and texture.

Fabrics
Any firm base fabric is suitable but it must be stretched in a frame or the fabric will pucker.

Threads
A wide variety of different types of yarn may be used to create different effects.

Needles
Tapestry or large-eyed wool needles should be used to suit the yarn.

Designs
Needleweaving designs tend to be fairly freeform, often with the base threads radiating from a central point.

Freestyle surface needleweaving

2 Single laid threads can be wrapped by winding the working thread round them.

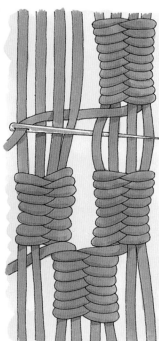

1 Using a fairly thick, strong yarn, such as pearl cotton, tapestry or knitting wool, work a series of long stitches either parallel to one another or radiating from a point. With a contrasting thread, weave under and over groups of the laid stitches, pulling them together or leaving the weaving untensioned to form flat areas of texture.

Beads and rings

The laid stitches may be threaded through large-holed beads, rings or washers as the work proceeds. Other beads can be added while weaving. For additional texture, back-stitched needleweaving, as for surface spider's web stitch (page 28), can also be included.

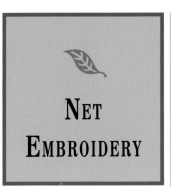

NET EMBROIDERY

Originally developed as a way to imitate lace, this delicate form of embroidery is not often seen today, mainly due to the intricacy involved in creating it. However, it is well worth trying as the results can be beautiful as well as dainty.

Fabrics
Hexagonal pattern nylon, cotton or silk net.

Threads
Fine sewing cotton or silk, which usually matches the colour of the net.

Needles
Fine tapestry needles.

Designs
The easiest to work are clearly defined designs that include outlined areas suitable for enriching with filling stitches. Geometric patterns and borders can also be incorporated.

◀ **Pamela Rooke**
Rock Pool Box
The main needlewoven elements are raised on small, rolled strips of felt. The hanging pieces are stitched in a similar way to woven picots.

Preparation

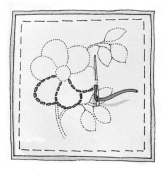

With a dark coloured felt tip pen, trace the outline of the design on to a sheet of stiff paper. The colour of the paper should contrast with that of the net. Tack the net in place over the design.

Stitching
Using a fine cotton or silk thread, work running stitches around the outline, darning in and out of the intersections of the net. To start and finish, darn the ends into the previously worked stitches as inconspicuously as possible.

▶ **Pauline Brown**
Honesty
The seed pods have been depicted by using appliquéd net and organza, with pattern darning.

Stitching filling patterns

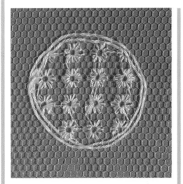
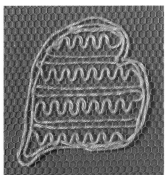

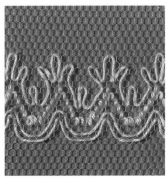

All fillings should be worked with as few joins as possible. The most commonly used stitches are running and back stitches, but eyelets and herringbone stitch can also be worked.

The sequence of stitching needs to be worked out before commencing, as, because of its transparency, the underside of the stitching will show through and be part of the finished effect.

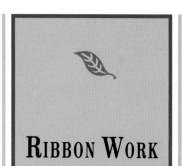

RIBBON WORK

There is a variety of ribbons on the market today – single and double-faced satins, velvet, grosgrain, brocade, check and printed types.

Their primary use is for trimmings. Apply them by machine stitching them down either flat, or ruched, gathered or pleated.

In addition, fine ribbons can be used as a type of embroidery thread for stitching on fabric or canvas, creating beautiful textures and decorative effects when used imaginatively.

Threads
For machine or hand appliqué use ordinary matching sewing thread.

Needles
Large-eyed tapestry or chenille needles are needed when using ribbons for embroidery.

Ribbon on fabric

Choose loosely woven fabric and fine 1.5- or 3-mm (¹⁄₁₆- or ⅛-in) wide ribbon, threaded in a blunt, large-eyed needle. Experiment with surface embroidery stitches, making sure that the ribbon does not twist unintentionally and spoil the stitch. To start and finish, secure the ends of the ribbon with a few stitches in cotton thread.

Ribbon on canvas

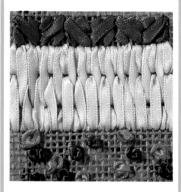

The width of the chosen ribbon should match the size of the holes in the canvas.

Most needlepoint stitches (pages 40 to 79) are suitable, but it is important that the ribbon lies flat without twisting.

Stitching ribbon by machine

Wide ribbon can be attached to backing fabric by top stitching along both edges, either with straight or zigzag stitches.

Narrow ribbons are best stitched using an open zigzag stitch, the width being set slightly wider than that of the ribbon.

Ribbons can also be gathered or ruched. To ruche, work a zigzag line of long stitches from edge to edge along the length of the ribbon. Draw up the gathers, then stitch the ruched ribbon in place.

◄ Caroline Birkett-Harris
This ribbon embroidery sampler displays a variety of stitches: feather stitch, French knots, herringbone, lazy daisy, fishbone, couching, running stitch, back stitch and fly stitch, as well as some ribbon weaving.

SHADOW WORK

Shadow work was popular in the 18th century when it was one of the fashionable whitework techniques.

Worked on transparent fabric, this method uses mainly close herringbone (or double back) stitch worked on the reverse side of the material, thereby producing a "shadowy" effect when viewed from the right side.

Fabrics
White or very pale transparent fabrics such as organza, organdie or very fine cotton are most suitable and should be stretched in a frame.

Threads
White or brightly coloured standard cotton or silk work best. Always test the depth of colour underneath the chosen fabric.

Needles
Fine embroidery needles produce the best results.

Designs
These should be small scale ones with simple outlines. The design can be traced directly onto the fabric.

Close herringbone stitch

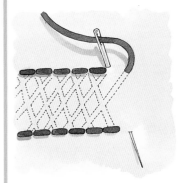

Also known as double backstitch, this is usually worked on the reverse side of the transparent fabric. It is similar to the surface embroidery close herringbone (page 21), with each stitch touching. This produces parallel lines of continuous stitches on the right side of the fabric with the "shadow" of the herringbone stitch showing through the fabric between them.

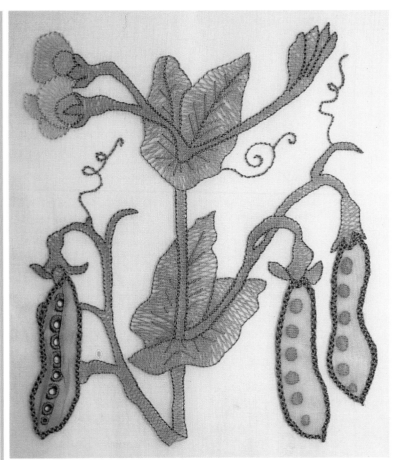

▲ **Kathryn Francis**
Pea Pods
The main leaves and flower are worked in double back stitch, the pea pods are depicted using appliqué and shadow appliquéd techniques.

SMOCKING

Best known as the charming traditional decoration on children's dresses, smocking is ideal for controlling and gathering fullness, but can also be used creatively to produce interesting textural effects.

Fabrics

It is usual to choose a fine material that will gather and drape well. When calculating the amount of fabric to buy allow about three times the width you want the finished piece of smocking to be. It is wise to work a small sampler in your chosen fabric before beginning as different fabrics gather more tightly or loosely than others.

Threads

For gathering, use strong sewing cotton in a contrasting colour to that of the background fabric. For the smocking, embroidery threads such as stranded cotton, coton à broder and pearl cotton are all suitable. Other yarns can be tried for experimental smocking.

Needles

Any embroidery needle that suits the thread may be used.

Designs

Traditional smocking is usually worked in horizontal bands across the garment. It is essential to count the number of gathers to work out the positioning of the various elements of the design, particularly for those stitches that create zigzags or diamonds.

Preparation

The fabric is gathered into vertical folds by working regular rows of running stitches across the straight grain of the fabric. Unless you own a smocking gathering machine, a grid of dots should be marked on the fabric prior to gathering to keep the stitches, and therefore the folds, uniform.

Marking the dots

1 Iron-on dot transfers are available. Position and pin the transfer face down on the wrong side of the fabric, so that the dots follow the grain. Press with a medium-hot iron.

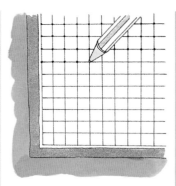

2 Alternatively, to make your own grid, place a piece of graph paper on the wrong side of the fabric with a sheet of dressmakers' carbon paper between. Mark a dot with a ballpoint pen at the appropriate measured intersection.

Gathering

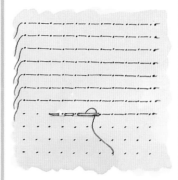

Thread the needle with a length of sewing cotton slightly longer than the width of the fabric. Knot the end and work even running stitches, picking up a tiny amount of fabric at each dot. Leave the thread hanging and start a new one for each row.

Pulling up and tying off

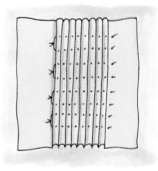

When all the rows have been completed, pull up the threads in pairs to the required width so that the folds lie evenly. Tie the pairs of threads together to hold the folds in place.

Stitching

Smocking is usually worked from left to right across the folds in the chosen pattern, with each stitch involving picking up a small amount of fabric at the centreline of the fold. To begin, the thread is brought through the first left-hand fold slightly to the left of the centreline and to finish, it is taken down to the right of the centreline of, and through, the last fold, fastening off with a double back stitch on the wrong side.

Stem and mock chain

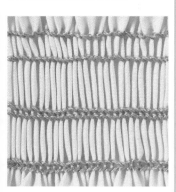

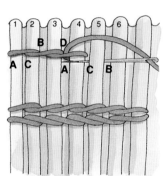

Stem (or outline) stitch is a tightly tensioned stitch, made in a similar way to surface embroidery stem stitch (page 16). Bring the needle up at A, take the thread over two folds, keeping it above the needle, then insert it at B and bring it out at C to repeat.

This can be reversed, and if two rows are worked close together, reversing the second, it produces mock chain stitch.

Cable stitch

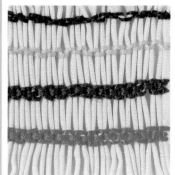

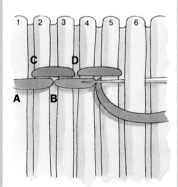

Make the first stitch over two folds as for stem stitch, keeping the thread above the needle. Make the next stitch with the thread below the needle over folds 2 and 3. Continue across the work, making stitches over two folds with the thread alternately above and below the needle. Double cable stitch consists of two rows of cable stitch in which the second row forms a mirror image of the first.

Wave and trellis stitches

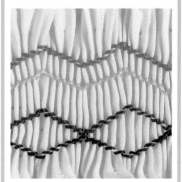

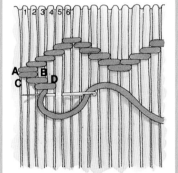

These are worked in zigzag formation in steps across the work. The stitches are similar to stem stitch, with the needle being slightly angled as it emerges above or below the thread. For the downward steps, the thread is kept above the needle and for the upward steps it remains below. Trellis stitch is formed by working two or more rows of wave stitch in opposite directions to create a diamond pattern.

Diamond stitch

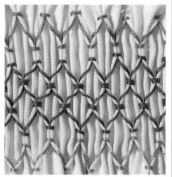

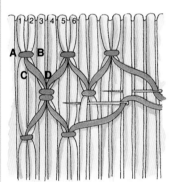

Work a stem stitch over two folds, keeping the thread above the needle and bringing the needle out between the folds. Take the thread down diagonally and insert the needle between folds 3 and 4. Work a stem stitch over folds 3 and 4 with the thread below the needle before taking it diagonally up to folds 5 and 6. Repeat.

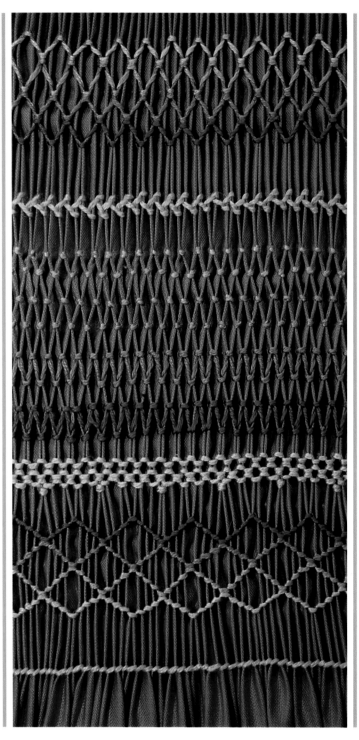

Surface honeycomb stitch

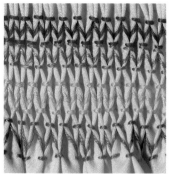

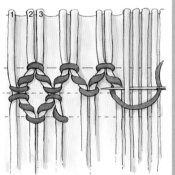

This is worked in a similar way to diamond stitch, but make the first stitch over folds 1 and 2 and the second over folds 2 and 3.

Honeycomb stitch

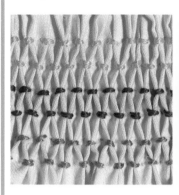

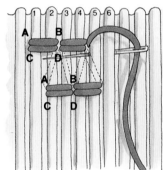

Using a double stitch, this groups the folds of fabric together in pairs to form a delicate cell-like appearance. Bring the needle out at A, insert it at B, picking up folds 2 and 1, then bring it out again at C, just below A. Repeat the stitch to D, but this time angle it down through the fold to the left-hand side of fold 2. Take the next set of double stitches over folds 2 and 3. Repeat, alternating the position of the double stitches to the end of the row.

◄ **Fiona Lewis**
Sampler with diamond, feather, surface honeycomb, honeycomb, double cable, trellis and stem stitches.

REVERSE SMOCKING

Reverse smocking differs from traditional smocking in that the stitches are worked on the back to form a textured surface.

A development of this technique is Canadian or North American smocking. It differs from the usual method of working in that the preparatory gathering is omitted and the fabric is ruched or pleated either from the front or the back of the work, depending on the design.

Fabrics
Reverse smocking is often used for cushion covers made from velvet or satin, but can be worked experimentally for textured articles and wallhangings in many different fabrics.

Threads
Strong thread, such as linen or button thread, that matches the fabric is used for picking up the marked dots and stitching them together to form the patterns.

Reverse smocking

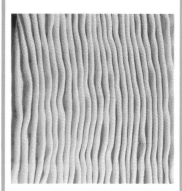

For reverse smocking, the gathered fabric is stitched from the back, using rows of stem stitch to preserve the folds so that no stitching is visible on the front.

Lattice pattern

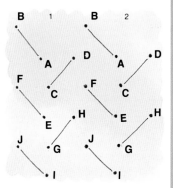

Mark out the grid on the wrong side of the fabric with a water-soluble pen. Using strong thread, knotted at one end, pick up a small amount of fabric at A; then pick up dot B, then dot A again, pulling A and B tightly together with a small stitch. Move down to C, keeping the thread slack between A/B and C. Pick up the dots at C and D, bringing them together before moving on to E. Continue down the length of the grid. Then work the second row, repeating across the width of the grid.

Flower pattern

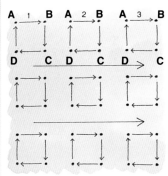

Mark the grid on the right side of the fabric. Pick up a small amount of fabric at A with a diagonal stitch, proceed to B, C and D and back to A. Pull the thread tightly, drawing the four corners of the square together and secure with a back stitch. Take the thread to the back of the work, ready to stitch the second square. Keep the fabric flat between each square.

STUMPWORK

Raised embroidery was always an integral part of the repertoire utilized in the ecclesiastical embroideries of the Middle Ages, but became more prominent in the 1600s when it was often stitched by young girls to form elaborate decoration for pictures, caskets and mirror frames.

Three-dimensional effects are very much a part of textile work today and so the techniques of stumpwork are still used as they are an ideal way of producing interesting results.

Fabrics
Any firm, closely woven background fabric can be used. It must be stretched in a frame to prevent distortion.

Threads
A variety of smooth-textured yarns, including stranded cotton, coton à broder and pearl cotton are all suitable.

Needles
Embroidery needles are usual, with tapestry needles being ideal for the detached stitches.

Designs
Although the designs of the past generally consisted of a series of motifs arranged in a haphazard fashion, today's embroiderers usually seek more integrated effects. Natural forms, such as fruit and flowers, figures and architectural features have all provided design ideas. The scale of stumpwork is usually fairly small, so the technique requires dexterity and good workmanship.

Stitches
The majority of stitches used to produce the raised effects of stumpwork are also found in other types of embroidery where their effect is likely to be less textured.

Particular stitches for stumpwork
Bullion knots (page 30). Detached buttonhole stitch (page 115). French knots (page 30). Padded satin stitch (page 24). Raised cup stitch (page 29). Tent stitch slips (page 40). Woven picots (page 27).

▲ **Barbara Hirst**
The Chiltern Farmer
The sheep is worked as a slip in pendant couching (page 17), with a padded, leather head. Needlelace (page 114) worked on a wire cordonnet creates the farmer's garments.

Slips

These are small motifs that are embroidered separately from the main design, then cut out and stitched in place. Needlepoint slips are usually worked in silk or wool in tent stitch on fine canvas.

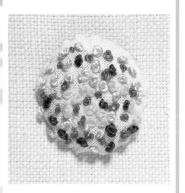

Small fabric slips are first embroidered with stitches such as French or bullion knots covering the surface. These are then usually padded and applied to the surface.

Padded appliqué

This type of padded shape differs from fabric slips in that the embroidery is done *after* the motif has been stitched in place. Work in a similar way to padded appliqué with turned edges (page 94) adding stitches to decorate.

Using craft interfacing

Cut out the motif in heavy craft interfacing and tack it lightly to the background fabric. Work satin stitch evenly to cover the interfacing. To do this, it may be helpful to begin at the middle of the motif, work outwards one way and then work from the centre out the other way to complete.

Freestanding wire shapes

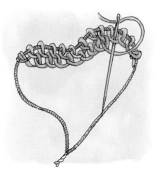

Cut a long enough length of fine florists' wire to encircle the shape and wrap it with stranded cotton. Start by tying the cotton to the wire and bending the end of the wire over it to hold it on. Wrap tightly and smoothly, finishing in the same way you started. Twist the ends of the wire together and bend to form the required shape. This can then be filled with a needlelace filling (page 115).

Modelling clay bases

Wooden moulds (the original "stumps" that gave stumpwork its name) were used as a basis for heads, figures, fruits and so on. A modern replacement is self-hardening modelling clay, which can be selected for its colour or completely covered with stitches or fabric. Before the clay hardens, make two or three small holes at the edges of the mould through which a securing stitch can be made to attach it to the background fabric.

Wrapping vellum

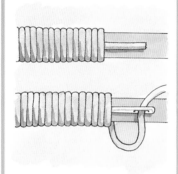

Although vellum was originally used for this technique, thin card or heavy craft interfacing make suitable substitutes.

Cut a narrow strip of vellum of the required length. Lay the end of a length of stranded cotton along the vellum, towards one end. Start wrapping the vellum evenly and smoothly until the whole length is covered. Thread the end of the cotton into a tapestry needle and bring it back through the wrapping to complete.

The wrapped lengths can be couched down in a variety of loops, twists or folds, which stand away from the surface.

▲ **Barbara Hirst**
Henry VIII
The head of this fine portrait has been soft sculptured from calico. The sumptuous clothing is created with needlelace, tiny Victorian beads, semi-precious stones and pearls, and bits of ostrich feather.

The embroideries of this talented stumpwork artist are always worked in threads no thicker than 100/3 silk.

Raised leaf stitch

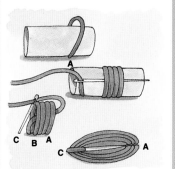

Cut a narrow strip of card about 0.5 × 5 cm (¼ × 2 in) to use as a template. Bring a needle threaded with pearl cotton up at A, alongside the card. Work six to eight satin stitches over the card, keeping it in an upright position on the surface of the fabric.

Bring the needle up at B and thread it through the stitches to the beginning. Remove the card carefully and pull the loops back, inserting the needle at C to produce a slightly raised leaf shape.

Banksia rose stitch

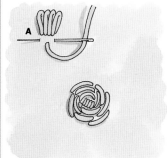

To form the centre of the rose, bring the needle out at A and take it down close by, leaving a small loop. Work several loops the same size close together with the last one secured with a back stitch. Then, work four loose stem stitches (page 16) encircling the loops. Continue working stem stitch, gradually decreasing the tension and increasing the number so that by the fourth row the rose is complete.

▼ **Barbara Hirst**
Samurai Three
This dramatic figure is clad in needlelace embellished with gold leather and gold machine threads and with fine beading wire worked as an integral part of the cordonnet. The head has been soft sculptured from calico.

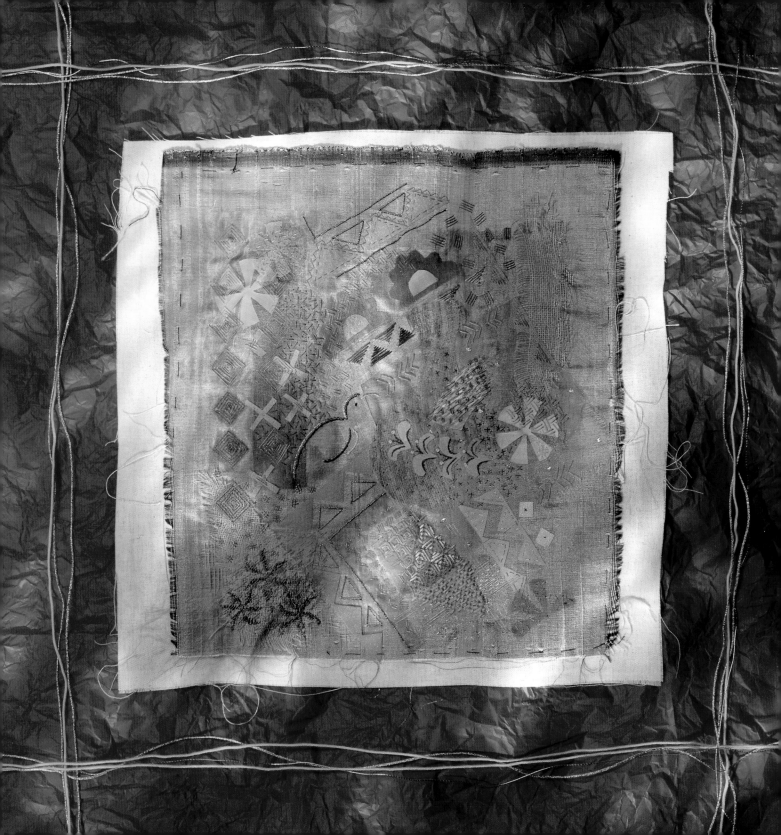

THEMES

Embroidery can be used to interpret different subjects in a variety of decorative styles, but the wide range of techniques, fabrics and threads also offers plenty of scope for developing an innovative personal style. Very often a new technique or an exciting fabric will spark off an idea for a project. Embroidery is so versatile that it can be used creatively for pictures and panels, for items for the home, for garments and accessories and also for three-dimensional objects. Studying the work of other embroiderers will enable you to see how other artists have interpreted a subject and give you the confidence to experiment.

LANDSCAPE

Painters have always been inspired by the landscape, whether it be a classic country view, a beautiful sunset or a dynamic seascape. For embroiderers, this source of subject matter has a similar appeal, with the added attraction that a wide range of techniques can be utilized in many different materials and threads, to create texture, depth and so on.

Designs for landscape, townscape, architecture or interiors can be sketched and notes made as to the colours, textures, mood and atmosphere of the scene. This will help you to determine the qualities you want to put across in the embroidery and give you ideas for the method, fabrics and thread to use. Alternatively, you can take your inspiration from photographs or other visual reference material. These can be modified and adapted to suit your preferences, the scale can be adjusted, colours changed and

certain aspects of the design accentuated or played down as you like.

The techniques used most often to create realistic depictions of landscapes are surface and machine stitches, together with fabric paints and appliqué.

Fabrics can be chosen to coincide with the textural qualities of the scene – for example, a heavily ribbed brown wool material can be used to depict furrows of a ploughed field, while a ruched silky fabric could be used to simulate the ripples of the sea.

Threads, too, may be chosen for their colour and texture and the direction in which the stitches are worked will have a bearing on the mood and realism of the piece.

For a somewhat more stylized effect, needlepoint and counted cross stitch are very popular. If the other counted thread methods are used, the result is usually more abstract.

◄ Pauline Brown
Herbaceous Border
18 × 25 cm (7 × 10 in)

An example of how combining freedom of approach with conventional needlepoint stitches can be very successful. Surface embroidery stitches, ribbons and appliqué are added for textural effect. The foxgloves are made from tiny rolled-up pieces of fabric and the foreground area includes three-dimensional leaves worked in Milanese stitch.

▼ Lydia Solomon
Cornfield
48 × 58 cm (19 × 23 in)

Fabric paints were used to create the sky and background before machine stitching the fields and fence posts. The foreground area is more densely stitched by hand, mainly using straight stitches, couching, bullion and French knots.

◄ Lydia Solomon
Home Thoughts from Abroad
47 × 56 cm (18½ × 22 in)

This realistic effect has been achieved by working over a fabric-painted background with machine-stitched whip and satin stitches. The blossom and foreground are mainly depicted with hand-worked French knots and straight stitch.

◄ **Anna Goad**
Images of the Orient II
29 × 20 cm (11½ × 8 in)

This is one of a number of pieces inspired by the exotic atmosphere of holidays in Morocco and Turkey. Transparent fabrics, nets and silks, are bonded and hand-stitched to a background of dyed silks, and handmade and dyed paper.

► **Anna Goad**
Images of the Orient III
29 × 20 cm (11½ × 8 in)

A visit to the Blue Mosque in Istanbul provided the inspiration for this piece, which superimposes stitched transparent fabrics on a background of handmade paper.

► **Wendy Lees**
The Fountain
51 × 35 cm (20 × 14 in)

The artist's aim when creating this layered fabric piece was to capture the fine spray in stitches and the mystical light against the background of dark trees. Beads, sequins and hand embroidery have their own special part to play in creating the right effect.

▲ **Elizabeth de Clermont**
Morris Hall with Peanut Playing
30 × 30 cm (12 × 12 in)

The inner picture of the
embroiderer's home is worked
in appliqué and the details are
picked out in surface stitches.
This is framed with a needlepoint border, mainly worked in
wools, with the trees wrapped
in gold and wool threads.

▼ **Margaret Pascoe**
Towers and Flowers
100 × 57 cm (39 × 22½ in)

The starting point for this blackwork embroidery was a newspaper cutting of the Lloyds building in London. The unusual way in which the technique is worked incorporates black threads of many thicknesses, plus coloured stranded cotton. The directions in which the stitches are worked give form to the shape of the building.

▶ **Ann Danielson**
Burning Stubble
33 × 40 cm (13 × 16 in)

This embroidery was inspired by seeing fields of burning stubble in the evening light. Strips of layered and frayed fabrics are sewn on a cotton base fabric. The Cretan stitch worked in a haphazard fashion successfully evokes the impression of the corn in the foreground.

▼ Ann Wheeler
Indian Palace
75 × 50 cm (29½ × 20 in)

This abstract hanging depicting a landscape is one of a series of pieces inspired by Indian architecture. Its muted, hand-dyed colours, and machine embroidery with metallic threads evoke an air of mystery.

◄ Margaret Pascoe
Three Trees
42 × 38 cm (16½ × 15 in)

Straight stitches worked in different directions—vertical, horizontal and diagonal—over counted threads produce variations in density and tonal value and break up the formality of the design.

▲ Alison King
Hillside, Amulree
90 × 75 cm (36 × 30 in)

The emotional atmosphere of this landscape has been captured by using a variety of different fabrics, including hand-dyed felts, and paper, some of which extend on to the mount. Machine embroidery provides texture and detail.

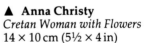 **▲ Anna Christy**
Cretan Woman with Flowers
14 × 10 cm (5½ × 4 in)

Inspired by the artist's drawn
and photographic reference,
this realistic embroidery was
achieved by using the stitches
and threads as if they were a
drawing medium. These
stitches are densely worked to
cover the background fabric
and the directions in which the
stitches are worked help to
create the different textures
that make up the scene.

▶ Margaret Burdett
Cyprus Valley (detail)
60 × 64 cm (23½ × 25 in)

The colours and textural
qualities of the bark of the
eucalyptus trees are depicted
by means of canvaswork in
wools and silks on a
background of dyed and
transparent fabrics. The
foreground area is worked in
quilting, using wrapped cane
and strips of balsa wood.

◀ **Jean Bow**
Summer Garden
51 × 44 cm (20 × 17 in)

Brown hessian sponged with dye provides an alternative to the fabrics conventionally used for pulled work. The garden scene is created by means of a range of eyelets, combined with satin stitch and a variety of other stitches. The work has been mounted on a strongly coloured blue lining which shows through the embroidery and gives an additional lift to the work.

▶ **Sara Norrish**
Greenhouse Doorway
60 × 40 cm (24 × 6 in)

Having completed a series of paintings of greenhouses, gardens and conservatories, the artist experimented with the theme in embroidery, resulting in this piece. Layers of fabrics, including chiffons, nets and scrims, were machine embroidered with various stitches, including free machining, cable and whip stitches, creating a lush, textured foreground.

PEOPLE AND ANIMALS

Depicting the human figure in embroidery can be a rather daunting prospect unless you are practised in life drawing. This is an obvious starting point and a sound foundation on which to base designs that are to have a degree of realism about them. For inexperienced artists, however, a simpler alternative is to use family photographs, holiday snapshots or magazine cuttings, all of which can provide suitable reference material for developing into successful designs.

The human form may be static or captured in movement. The right treatment will depend on the degree of detail required – whether it is depicted in close-up, at a distance or simply in silhouette.

Faces and heads, including masks, make interesting subjects, especially when they are carried out in a decorative or stylized manner.

Producing caricatures can be a delightful way of overcoming the difficulty of depicting the face or figure realistically, and this treatment can also

be used for designs based on animals.

The animal world offers a wealth of subject matter, from domestic pets to wild animals. Also included in this category are butterflies, insects, birds and fish, many of which have interesting patterns and textures that are easy to depict in embroidery.

Sketching animals is likely to be difficult as they generally do not stay still for very long, but designs can be developed from photographs or reference books on natural history.

There is no restriction on the techniques suitable for developing designs based on people and animals. Some of the raised and padded techniques, such as appliqué, quilting and stumpwork offer the chance to create designs in high- or low-relief, giving form to the subject.

Designs which include some of the more decorative birds, fish or insects can be worked using intricate surface stitchery, needlepoint, metal thread work or counted thread techniques.

◀ **Wendy Lees**
Boy with Two Ice-creams
47 × 35 cm (18½ × 14 in)

Recreated from photographic reference material, the effect of the running boy has been developed by using a series of straight stitches on a foundation of appliquéd chiffons and nets. The silhouetted figure in the background counterbalances that of the main subject.

◀ **Janet Haigh**
The Whitaker Family
90 × 50 cm (36 × 20 in)

This commissioned sampler contains imagery of people, animals and places important to the owner. Many different types of embroidery have been used, making it a sampler for the artist as well as the client. These include appliqué, needlepoint, beadwork, crewel and counted thread embroidery in a wide variety of fabrics and threads.

▶ **Wendy Lees**
Boy Seated
140 × 108 cm (55 × 43 in)

Taken from a pastel drawing of a model at a life class, this machine-quilted wallhanging has been created from plain-coloured cotton fabrics. These have been further strengthened by the outlines of the black background which shows between the appliquéd fabrics.

▲ **Rose Verney**
Radha and Krishna
180 × 180 cm (72 × 72 in)

Part of a set which was commissioned to hang over a bed, this hand-pieced appliqué relies for its effect on the strength of the figures and surrounding decor contrasted with the black background. Details have been embroidered by hand with beads and jewels added.

▶ **Liz Harding**
Crocodile
60 × 92 cm (23½ × 36 in)

This charming embroidery was based on a postcard of Ethiopian children. Layers of soft cotton and felt have been stitched together with running stitches. Coloured cotton and silk fabrics have been appliquéd with hand and machine stitching.

◄ **Gisela Banbury**
Mother and Child
64 × 45 cm (25½ × 18 in)

The arrival of a baby in the family prompted this stylized version of a well-loved subject. An appliquéd background in strips of different fabrics serves as a foil for the figures, which are also appliquéd. The faces are treated in a simple but effective way with a minimum of hand and machine stitchery.

► **Karen Howse**
Procession
60 × 25 cm (24 × 10 in)

A trip to north India influenced this mixed media work, which brings together fragments of machine embroidery linked with pieces of wire and cane. The aim in creating this embroidery is to conjure up a textile "icon" which is rich in colour and textural variety.

▼ **Janet Haigh**
Clarice Cliff
46 × 30 cm (18 × 12 in)

The designs of a well-known decorator of pottery inspired this appliqué picture. The figure stands in a "landscape" of typical motifs taken from her china. Parts of this decorative background have been hand-painted and enhanced with surface stitches.

▲ **Karen Howse**
Three Monks (detail)

A mixed media piece in the
same series as "Procession"
(page 141). The three, robed
figures are set in a mystical
landscape.

◀ **Sonda Galsworthy**
Statue of Liberty
20 × 26 cm (8 × 10 in)

This interpretation in blackwork uses a variety of conventional stitches and the emphasis on the tonal values in the design gives form to the figure. Outlines are only used in some areas to strengthen the shapes.

◀ **Yvonne Morton**
Celestial Serpent
24 × 15 cm (9½ × 6 in)

The winged serpent presides over the heavens – the sun, moon and stars – in this decorative piece, which combines richly painted fabrics for the appliqué and quilting with free machining.

▲ **Belinda Montagu**
Domus
2.6 × 3.68 m (12 × 10 ft)

The first of four wallhangings commissioned by Lord Montagu which depict the history of Beaulieu Abbey, this is a multimedia piece. It was made in sections and then assembled. The faces and many of the birds and animals were worked in needlepoint, while other techniques used include patchwork, appliqué, quilting, machine embroidery and couched gold threads.

▼ **Ailsa M. Findlay**
Frieze from a Temple in Ankor Watt, Cambodia
70 × 120 cm (27 × 48 in)

Based on a rubbing of the Cambodian temple frieze, this example of hand appliqué on linen employs a wide variety of fabrics, plus other components, such as feathers, lace, cord, leather, wood and string.

▶ **Morag Gilbert**
Silly Cow
30 × 30 cm (12 × 12 in)

A commissioned piece, it is a play on words. The image was drawn by free machining on the wool background. Details were than added by hand stitching in cotton and silk to give colour and form to the piece.

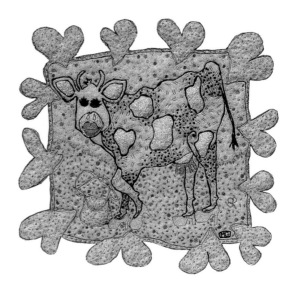

▼ **Niamh McCarthy**
Brent Geese
29 × 20 cm (11½ × 8 in)

The annual arrival of the geese from Greenland for their winter sojourn in Dublin sparked off the idea for this needlepoint piece. The interesting use of Bargello stitch, worked on the diagonal, produces the wonderful winter sky. Leaf stitch creates the effect of feathers, while Jacquard, Milanese and fan stitch are used for the other parts of the birds.

▶ **Elspeth Kemp**
Dove Ascending (detail of altar frontal)

Metal thread embroidery is often used for ecclesiastical embroidery because of its richly decorative effect. Here it is combined with appliqué and couching in a symmetrical design. The body of the bird is worked in basket stitch over a foundation of string; the rest of the raised areas are padded with felt.

▲ **Belinda Montagu**
Firescreen
75 × 60 cm (30 × 24 in)

A combination of techniques was used to make this embroidery intended for use as a firescreen. The ducks were first stitched on canvas and then appliquéd to the background, which had been prepared with machine appliqué and surface embroidery.

FLOWERS AND PLANTS

This subject area has long been a favourite with embroiderers. The Elizabethans, Stuarts and Georgians decorated their garments with detailed floral motifs and the Victorians embroidered posies, wreaths and sprays of flowers on all manner of household items as well as clothing.

Collecting reference material is particularly simple. Whether you live in a town or the country, parks, gardens or flower stalls are all close at hand for personal study and a visit to the library will provide books with botanical illustrations. Gardening magazines and seed catalogues are easily obtainable and often give good close-up photographs.

Flowers can be embroidered in a realistic fashion with attention to detail, shading and form, or you may prefer to treat them in an impressionistic or stylized way, while still capturing the essence and unique characteristic of

each particular species.

For a middle-distance view of a group of plants, look particularly at the movement, rhythm and direction of growth, as well as the overall shape and textural quality.

Surface embroidery is probably the most popular method for depicting flowers realistically, but this is by no means the only way in which such effects can be achieved. The smooth texture of freestyle machine embroidery will create equally convincing realism and the use of multicoloured and *ombré* threads can produce the necessary subtle shading. Three-dimensional effects can be achieved by using wired needlelace and stumpwork techniques, or individual flowers can be fashioned from pieces of fabric cut to shape. Needlepoint, crewel and laid work are ideal for creating stylized designs, and cutwork and other whitework techniques are often used to good effect for floral subjects.

◀ **Gila Mader**
Summer Garden (detail)

The rich texture combined
with strong colour are the main
features of this wool
embroidery. Stitches used
include knots, couching and
straight stitches, with rolls and
strips of felt attached by hand.

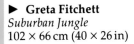

▶ **Greta Fitchett**
Suburban Jungle
102 × 66 cm (40 × 26 in)

The richly coloured
background for this
wallhanging was hand-dyed
and machine embroidered.
The free-standing flowers and
leaves were created by
machining on dissolvable
fabric and then appliquéing
them to the background.

▲ **Greta Fitchett**
Delphiniums
92 × 66 cm (36 × 26 in)

The velvet background throws the lighter colours of the appliquéd satins and sheers into sharp contrast. Texture is provided by means of buttons, surface and machine stitchery, together with Suffolk puffs (small motifs made from gathered circles of fabric).

◄ **Sarah W. Mitchell**
Reflections
60 × 66 cm (24 × 26 in)

The interesting composition of
this piece relies for its effect
on the differing scale of the
four jigsaw areas. A variety of
fabrics and threads have been
incorporated, with a
combination of hand and
machine stitches being used.
The poppies in the foreground
are made from manipulated
silk with hand stitching, while
the large bloom is made from
painted silk.

◄ **Daphne J. Ashby**
Poppies and Daisies
18 × 13 cm (7 × 5 in)

Solidly worked free machine
embroidery on cotton, using a
variety of threads, creates a
realistic effect. French knots
worked in the centres of the
flowers complete the picture.

► **Daphne J. Ashby**
Hellebore Niger
43 × 36 cm (17 × 14 in)

This successful combination
of techniques includes a
needlepoint background, a
variety of other stitches and
French knots, plus appliquéd
flowers and leaves made from
silk with beads and stitches
added to complete the effect.

◀ Barbara Walters
Sunflowers
44 × 44 cm (17 × 17 in)

This is one of a series of sunflower pictures worked after a visit to France. Mono-printed fabric was cut up and appliquéd to a painted background, and then machine embroidery was densely worked over this.

 ▶ Sandra Grant
Lilies
70 × 25 cm (27½ × 10 in)

A free-form representation of orange lilies, the piece was created in a similar way to 'Yellow Tulips'' (right).

▲ Sandra Grant
Yellow Tulips
40 × 50 cm (16 × 20 in)

This stunning depiction of realistic three-dimensional tulips is stitched to a background made from layers of fine fabrics machined together with coloured threads, the stitching creating a painterly effect. The tulips and leaves are wired to give them their shape and attached to wired and wrapped stalks.

▼ Anita Faithfull
Painted Waistcoat

Using her garden as a source of inspiration, the artist has captured the many shades of the leaves by using silk paints on habutai silk, which she has then quilted by machine using a shiny thread. The vibrancy of the leaves contrasts with the painted and machine-stitched geometric design of the background.

▲ **Maggie Phillips**
Water Garden
35 × 35 cm (14 × 14 in)

Painted linen forms the basis
of the watery background here
with appliquéd nets and
tarlatan. Machine embroidery
creates the vegetation. The
needlepoint mount is worked
with Rhodes, tent and straight
Gobelin stitches.

▶ **Pamela Rooke**
Clematis Montana
20 × 20 cm (8 × 8 in)

The geometric pattern of the
transfer-painted background,
which represents an open-
work screening wall, acts as a
contrast to the natural forms of
the clematis. The flower
shapes are worked in layers of
fabric with gold metal thread
embroidery.

◀ Margaret Griffiths
Jardinière
47 × 47 cm (18 × 18 in)

For this well-loved subject, a number of hand and machine-stitched techniques have been incorporated on a painted background. The vase has been trapunto-quilted and the butterflies have been worked in machine-made lace. Stitches include French knots, woven wheels and needleweaving in a variety of different threads.

▼ Peggy Field
The Yellow Carpet
76 × 76 cm (30 × 30 in)

The interesting background of this piece was achieved by spray-dyeing around hand-made templates on to four layers of organdie, which were then machine embroidered. The vase is appliquéd and the flowers are mainly worked in long, straight hand stitches.

ABSTRACTS

Abstract designs can be developed from almost any source. Realistic images can be adapted, reduced or embellished so that the result only vaguely resembles the original form. Abstract patterns can also be based on geometric shapes, lines or random motifs. Embroidery designs can arise from doodles and "accidental" designs, such as ink blots or reflections in puddles or shadows. These may be rhythmic and flowing, rigid or spiky with colours which can be changed to reflect your personality – indeed emotions, moods and abstract feelings can all be linked to particular colours, textures and shapes. Many embroiderers gain inspiration from the embroidery materials themselves, producing work which

relies mainly on colour or texture for its effect.

Some of the counted thread techniques, such as Hardanger and drawn thread work, rely for their impact on the strong abstract geometric forms which are inherent in their construction. Pulled work, blackwork and counted cross stitch can also be used for abstract designs.

The freedom of machine embroidery is particularly suited to abstraction – drawing in a random fashion with the needle can produce an interesting starting point which can be developed further as the work progresses.

Appliquéd and quilted fabrics, haphazardly arranged, make a good basis on which to stitch freely, resulting in highly textured and colourful pieces.

▼ **Corliss Miller**
Elizabethan Frame
23 × 25 cm (9 × 10 in)

Potato and sponge prints in gold and pearlized acrylic paints have been appliquéd to this highly decorative quilted and machine-embroidered piece. The design was based on a study of the costume and embroidery of the Elizabethan period.

◄ **Avril Lansdell**
Treasure Hoard
22 × 17 cm (8½ × 7 in)

This small piece displays a formal approach to spider's web stitch. It is based on a chain stitch grid, containing stitches and pieces of appliquéd fabrics.

▲ **Karen Howse**
Midsummer Shade
20 × 33 cm (8 × 13 in)

In this constructed piece, which uses images of India as a starting point, a series of machine-embroidered elements have been assembled. Cane, wire and beads are successfully used in combination with fabric and thread.

◀ Cynthia Pearson
Flower Patch II
46 × 46 cm (18 × 18 in)

Using a background of cotton velvet, the centre of the piece was built up by means of layers of machine stitching. The aim is to convey an impression of the green, lawned areas often found in suburban gardens in conjuction with the rich strong colours of summer flowers.

▶ Helen Collinson
Quilted Butterfly Garden
45 × 45 cm (18 × 18 in)

This immaculate work, based on a Japanese temple garden, combines a variety of techniques, including machine and hand quilting, shadow quilting and appliqué. The design has been carefully conceived to include a number of different patterns.

▶ Avril Lansdell
Seashore
23 × 30 cm (9 × 12 in)

This panel shows the use of spider's web stitch in a semi-abstract work. A patchwork of thin fabrics was diagonally quilted and the variety of stitches used gives the impression of a sandy beach with wooden groynes and a rock pool.

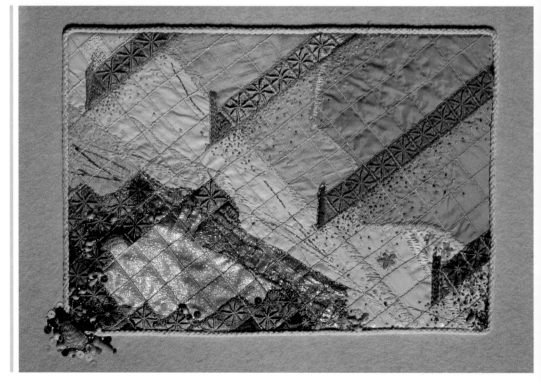

▲ **Hellen Collinson**
Quilted Butterfly Garden (detail)

A close-up view of this Japanese-influenced embroidery clearly shows the techniques used, including the appliquéd butterflies and couched cords.

◄ **Helen Collinson**
Salmon and Gold Square (detail)

Balance and proportion are key elements in the design of this piece, which includes Japanese papers, fabric-covered card and wrapping techniques. The harmonizing colours are offset by the lustre of the gold threads, which create texture and interest.

◄ Vanessa Blackmoor
Her Passage Through the Trees
44 × 48 cm (17½ × 19 in)

Thinking about an "Alice in Wonderland" theme led to the idea of creating an image that would represent Alice's transition between the ordinary and dream worlds. The central hand-stitched panel is surrounded by a patchwork of different fabrics.

▼ Judy Hope
Rocks and Crystals
15 × 10 cm (6 × 4 in)

Photographs of underground caves prompted a series of embroideries in different techniques. For this example, hand-dyed felt circles were stitched with herringbone and Cretan stitch to the painted and textured background.

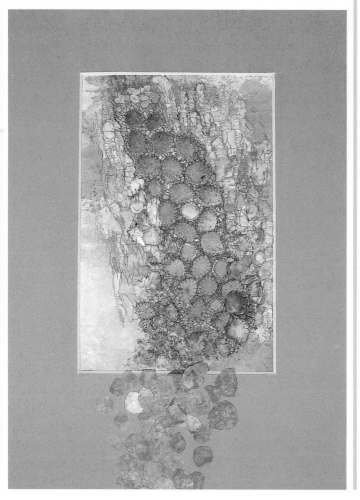

▲ Helen Pincus
Mordent
33 × 26 cm (13 × 10 in)

Based on musical forms, selected widths of card and rods have been hand-wrapped with knitting ribbon and then couched in place on an aluminium mesh base.

◄ Yvonne Morton
Byzantine II (detail)

A study of Byzantine architecture prompted a series of embroideries in richly quilted fabrics, layers of which were built up, painted and stitched to achieve this sumptuous effect.

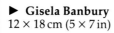
► Gisela Banbury
12 × 18 cm (5 × 7 in)

A variation on the ''spark plug'' theme (right), this repeat needlepoint piece in stranded and pearl cotton contains a variety of stitches including tent, cross, upright cross, Smyrna and Gobelin.

► **Charlotte Hodge**
Sundance
44 × 80 cm (17 × 32 in)

The impact of the vibrant colours is an integral part of this hand-stitched appliquéd piece. The frayed edges of the pieces of silk and the transparency of others add detail to the bold effect.

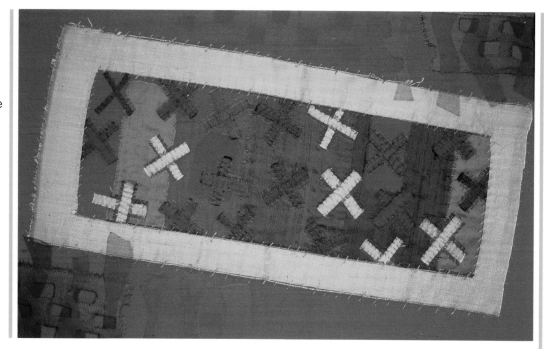

◄ **Gisela Banbury**
24 × 16 cm (9½ × 6 in)

Repeat geometric designs may be evolved from many different sources. The original inspiration for this Hardanger embroidery was a drawing of the top of a spark plug.

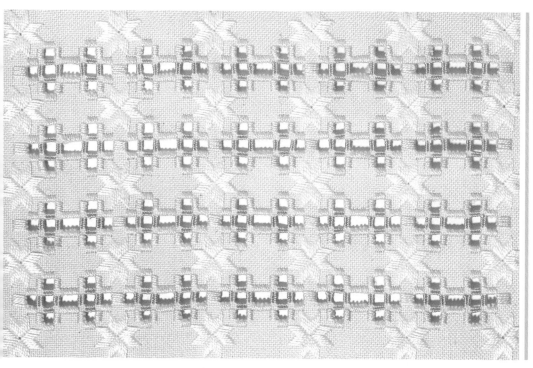

OBJECTS AND GARMENTS

One of the great advantages of embroidery is that it is so versatile. Not only can the various techniques be used for creating pictures, panels and decorative wallhangings, but they can be adapted for use on garments and accessories, as well as being used to decorate three-dimensional objects.

To use embroidery on garments was, in the past, the prerogative of the rich, but, today, quilted and machine-embroidered garments have become readily available. Embroiderers, though, are able to create out-of-the-ordinary designs for use on clothes simply to add individuality.

Accessories such as bags and belts readily lend themselves to being embellished with embroidery, and small items such as brooches, pendants and buckles can also be stitched. An innovation in embroidery is to make and decorate three-dimensional, constructed pieces. These can be totally abstract or realistically simulate natural or manmade forms.

When using embroidery for garments, thought

needs to be given to the use to which the article will be put. Machine appliqué and quilting are hardwearing and therefore suitable for everyday clothing and children's wear but beading and fine delicate work would be more appropriate for infrequently worn items, such as an evening dress.

Bags of all types can be embroidered and the same consideration as to use applies. Needlepoint would be hardwearing for a handbag or shopping bag, while evening bags embellished with beads and surface stitches can be embroidered to complement evening wear.

Small three-dimensional pieces of jewellery, made using machine embroidery or lace, can be fashioned for a delicate effect; more substantial pieces can be embroidered and stiffened to make them more robust.

For three-dimensional articles, foundations of card or wood can be covered with previously embroidered fabrics; padded, appliquéd shapes can be wired so that they become free-standing, and machine lace using dissolvable fabrics can be stiffened to hold its shape.

◀ Judy Clayton
Embroidered Bowl
25 × 18 cm (10 × 7 in)

The bubbly texture is achieved by using transparent plastic, silks, sequin waste and metallic threads, machine embroidered with whip stitch on a base of fabric dissolvable in hot water. This is shrunk and moulded to form the shape.

▼ Juliet Walker
Hand-held Fan
46 cm (18 in) in diameter

The colours and textures of this piece were inspired by marine life. Handmade paper has been combined with machine embroidery and a machine lace edging. Beads and sequins give additional sparkle and texture.

◀ Karen Holt
Brooch 2
13 × 9 cm (5 × 3½ in)

Scraps of fabrics are densely machine embroidered on a calico base with the outlines in braid. The embroidery is backed with heavy interfacing, so that it holds its shape, and then varnished to make it rigid.

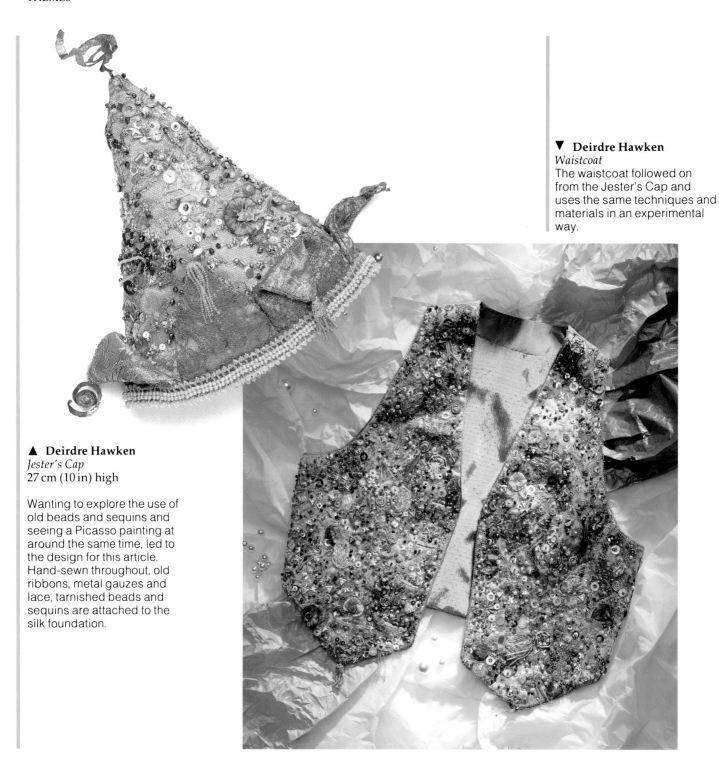

▼ **Deirdre Hawken**
Waistcoat
The waistcoat followed on from the Jester's Cap and uses the same techniques and materials in an experimental way.

▲ **Deirdre Hawken**
Jester's Cap
27 cm (10 in) high

Wanting to explore the use of old beads and sequins and seeing a Picasso painting at around the same time, led to the design for this article. Hand-sewn throughout, old ribbons, metal gauzes and lace, tarnished beads and sequins are attached to the silk foundation.

Janet Morris
Pisces waistcoat (detail)

Layered fine fabrics are combined with surface stitchery, including needleweaving and some beading. The motifs are made from crystal organza bonded to satin.

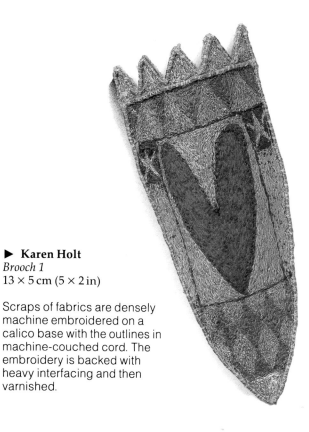

▶ Karen Holt
Brooch 1
13 × 5 cm (5 × 2 in)

Scraps of fabrics are densely machine embroidered on a calico base with the outlines in machine-couched cord. The embroidery is backed with heavy interfacing and then varnished.

▼ Karen Holt
Boot
18 × 31 × 9 cm (7 × 12 × 4 in)

One of a pair, this machine-embroidered boot is worked on a calico base, heavily stitched with metalic threads, scraps of fabric, couched cords and beads.

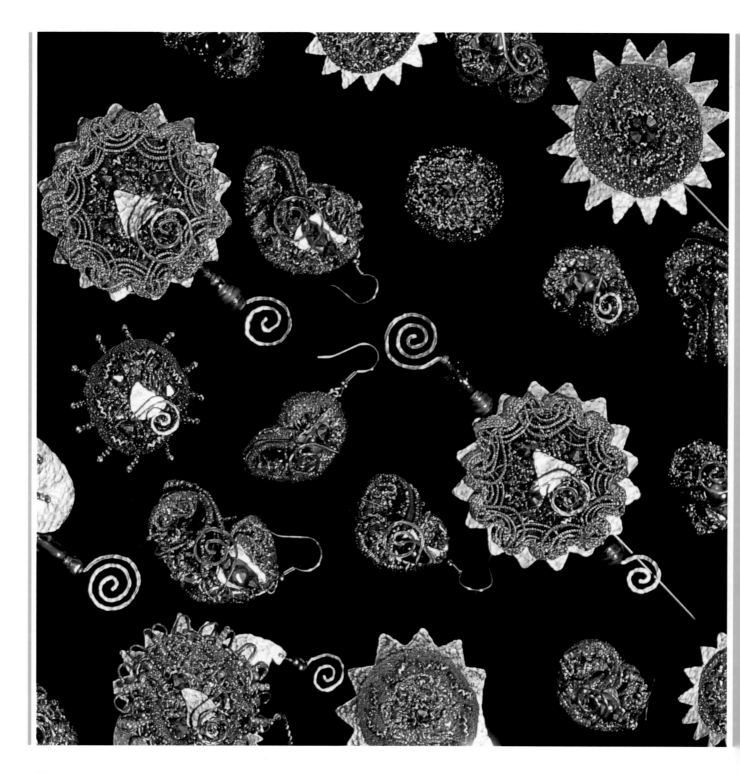

◀ **Judy Clayton**
Embroidered Jewellery
25 × 18 cm (10 × 7 in)

Made in a similar way to the
embroidered bowl (page 163),
this technique resulted from
the search for an embroidery
material that is not fragile and
suitable for three-dimensional
work.

▶ **Clare Hutchinson**
Sheherezade III
13 cm (5 in) in diameter

This bag, constructed from
hand-made felt, was an
Islamic-inspired pattern
worked in embroidery and
beads. A plaited silk braid for
the strap and a knotted silk
tassel with beads make
complementary finishing
trimmings.

▶ **Jean K. Fryer**
*"The World is a Stage" Jewellery
Box*
13 × 10 × 5 cm (5 × 4 × 2 in)
(closed)

A constructed piece inspired
by a love of theatre and the
desire to create a box which
contains an element of
surprise. Machine-
embroidered silk with applied
metallic fabrics and
distressed chiffon are laced
over thick card. Dissolvable
machine lace is used for the
pop-up characters and a
wearable stick-pin completes
the effect.

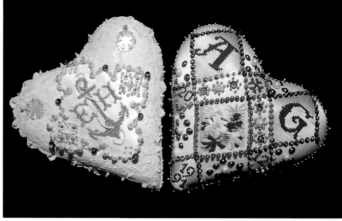

▲ **Janet Haigh**
Pincushions
15 × 15 cm (6 × 6 in)

Stuffed with perfumed
sawdust and stuck with beads
threaded on to pins, these
pincushions incorporate
hand-embroidered sections
with counted cross and long
and short stitch.

▲ **Abigail Mill**
Springtime print tray
23 × 37 cm (9 × 14 in)

A progression of flowerheads
– from bud to full flower and,
thence, to decay and seed
pods – are set in the compart-
ments of the print tray to
create a jewel-like effect.
Machine lace on cold-water-
soluble fabric incorporates
shot silks and velvets, metallic
organzas and threads.

▲ **Harriet C. Robinson**
Lily Bowls
11 × 11 × 5 cm (4 × 4 × 2 in)

Machine embroidery on
dissolvable fabric created
these small bowls. Each one
incorporates small scraps of
fabric held in place with plain
and metallic threads.

Glossary

Amager embroidery Silk thread work on silk scarves from the Danish island of Amager.

Arraiolos work Portuguese rug embroidery, usually worked in wool on linen.

Ayrshire embroidery 19th-century whitework technique incorporating surface stitches and needlelace fillings.

Beetlewing embroidery Introduced in the 19th century, it is metal thread embroidery, originating in South East India, used for decorating garments and household articles for the export market.

Berlin woolwork A 19th-century needlepoint technique, usually worked in tent stitch and sometimes including beads.

Carrickmacross lace From the Irish town of that name, fine cotton appliqué on net, stitched to resemble lace.

Casalguidi embroidery Italian whitework consisting of a pulled work background with raised motifs superimposed on it.

Crivos Portuguese raised whitework embroidery with bullion knots and drawn threads.

Deerfield embroidery Blue and white linen work from New England, similar to crewel embroidery.

Dorset feather stitchery Paisley-type designs built up in feather and buttonhole stitch. Often combined with traditional smocking.

Double-sided embroidery Worked on a vertical frame by two embroiderers, satin stitch is worked in such a way that both sides are the "right side".

Filet darning A form of decorating square mesh net with weaving in cotton or linen.

Hawaiian appliqué A combination of appliqué and quilting with bold designs representing traditional Hawaiian flowers and plants.

Hedebo embroidery Danish drawn thread work of intricate design, combining cutwork and needlelace fillings.

Inlay A type of appliqué in which one fabric is inlaid in another to form a completely flat surface.

Jacobean embroidery Style of crewel embroidery dating from the early 17th century.

Kantha embroidery Quilting from Bangladesh that incorporates colour and traditional patterns.

Lacis See filet darning.

Leek embroidery Ecclesiastical embroidery worked on printed fabric.

Levkara Cypriot whitework embroidery similar to Hardanger.

Madeira work Cutwork on fine cotton, often with the addition of appliqué.

Mountmellick work Heavy white cotton embroidery originating in Ireland.

Needlepainting Realistic embroidered pictures, often based on paintings.

Petit point Needlepoint embroidery worked entirely in tent stitch.

Phulkari embroidery Punjabi satin stitch worked in geometric patterns.

Ruskin work Linen cutwork popularized by John Ruskin in England's Lake District.

San Blas appliqué Reverse appliqué technique introduced by the Cuna Indians of San Blas, Panama.

Soutache embroidery Narrow braid appliqué.

Stained glass appliqué Appliqué resembling stained glass using bias strips to represent the leadwork.

Tambour work A hooked chain stitch method often used commercially for applying beads and sequins.

Telemark embroidery Bold floral woollen stitchery from Norway.

Turkeywork Raised pile stitch resembling velvet.

Whitework Any form of white on white embroidery.

INDEX

ACKNOWLEDGMENTS

In addition to all the embroiderers who have so kindly submitted examples of their work for this book, Quarto would like to thank both Elizabeth Elvin and Jayne Bleby at The Royal School of Needlework and Dorothy Tucker at the Embroiderers' Guild for their invaluable help in compiling this book.

Contact the Royal School of Needlework at Apartment 12a, Hampton Court Palace, East Molesey, Surrey KT8 9AU, and the Embroiderers' Guild at Apartment 41, Hampton Court Palace (as above).

Quarto would like to thank Kreinik and Coats Patons Crafts for their generosity in supplying thread for the book.

Coats Patons Crafts, McMullen Rd, Darlington, Co. Durham DL1 1YQ, U.K.

Kreinik Mfg. Co., Inc., P.O. Box 1966, Parkersburg, WV 26102, U.S.A.

Quarto would also like to thank Margaret Cooter for the Index and Anna Christy for supplying the example of work shown on pages 128–9.